CONFLICT AT WORK

A toolkit for managing your emotions for successful results.

Dr. M. Paula Daoust

Conflictatworkbook.com

Conflict at Work: A toolkit for managing your emotions for successful results.

Dr. M. Paula Daoust

Copyright © 2020 Maplewheat Publishing
Cover design: Germancreative

Editor: Frieda Paton

Assistant Editors: Dorissa Daoust and Pamela Brisendine

First Printing: September 2020

ISBN-13: **978-1-7353697-0-9**

Dr. M. Paula Daoust
Behavior Transitions

10940 Parallel Pkwy, Suite K-182

Kansas City, KS 66109

(785) 633-6078

www.BehaviorTransitions.com

www.ConflictatWorkBook.com

Dr. M. Paula Daoust is available to speak at your business or conference event on a variety of topics. Call (785) 633-6078 for booking information.

Why Read This Book

I have coached hundreds of leaders at all levels of various organizations. Using validated and reliable assessment tools, I have found that 85% of these leaders struggle with conflict management. When conflict is not handled well, there are serious consequences for careers and organizations' bottom-line.

Most people are not good at a skill that is critical to their job! Even when they attend training, their skill does not improve. Why? Because conflict is an emotional experience and not a rational, logical event. If your goal is to get better outcomes when dealing with conflict and you are like most people, you probably need some help in learning to manage your emotions. This book is packed full of tools that you can use today to make a difference in your career. Like a buffet, you can pick and choose the tools that feel most comfortable for you or will fit best with your situation. When you put together a plan that feels right for you, you will get those better outcomes you need and want.

Are you ready to differentiate yourself?

Do you want to be much better at something that matters to your work and to your life?

This book shows you how!

Conflict is an emotional event. Learn some simple tools that will guide your emotions so that you can get the results you need and want.

Additional free resource material for this book is available at:

https://conflictatworkbook.com/resources/

Conflict at Work

Written by a leading expert in performance management with over 40 years of experience

Dr. M. Paula Daoust has a doctorate in Behavior Psychology and is an expert in helping people find and maintain their peak performance. She is also a certified hypnotherapist and seamlessly blends these tools into her coaching to help people easily achieve lasting change. Over a period of 25 years, she has taught hundreds of master-level students how to be more persuasive and influential, and how to successfully manage conflict.

Dr. M. Paula Daoust is the expert other leaders look to for help in finding their peak performance. She has taught workshops and spoken at events all over North America on subjects such as conflict, change management, storytelling, influence and power, anxiety and stress at work and peak performance.

Do you want Dr. M. Paula Daoust to be the motivational speaker at your next event?

Call (785) 633-6078

or visit BehaviorTransitions.com

What others are saying
about this book

"I've known Paula for more than a decade, and there's no one I trust more to provide wisdom and guidance in the workplace. This book will help you get through those difficult moments at work stronger and better than before."

– Matt All,
President and CEO, Blue Cross and Blue Shield of Kansas

Conflict at Work is more than just another book about conflict management. It's an opportunity for us to really reflect over how we react when stakes are high and communication breaks down. It's a deep dive into the human condition when it comes to conflict – and the best part? It gives us tangible strategies to overcome what's holding us back from reaping the benefits of true candor and healthy disagreement. Dr. Daoust provides a mix of expansive knowledge of psychology, and decades of practical experience helping leaders in organizations address conflict in the workplace. The successes (and failures) she shares in Conflict at Work serve as an invaluable guide for anyone ready to take on the challenge of conflict management.

– Melia Stockham,
PhD, Professional Coach & Consultant,
Co-Founder of FLIGHT Leadership

Paula takes the complexity of conflict and provides individuals a new perspective into how their personal stories may or may not align with facts, causing blockage to better results. She helps to find meaning vs just managing conflict, providing a way forward to prepare, plan and execute"

– Jackie Grant,
Director of Client Solutions, The Ken Blanchard Companies

If you want to stay healthy, you need to do more than eat right and exercise. You need to take care of your emotional health as well and Conflict at Work is a great tool for doing just that.

– Zonya Foco,
RDN, Speaker, Author, Nutritionist, TV Host

Table of Contents

1

Whole-Brain Conflict Management

Are you good at dealing with conflict? Or are you like most – damaging an important relationship while trying to address the issue, or maybe, giving in and not getting what you need or want? Either outcome is unacceptable. It doesn't have to be like that.

The problem is that very few of us have learned effective tools to escape this either/or situation. When faced with conflict, most of us are still using the same tools we used as children, just a little more sophisticated. We engage in any or many of the following: tantrums, avoidance, badgering, overwhelming the other person with justifications, whining, complaining, appealing to a third party, demanding, crying, and on and on. These tactics either don't work or they work only marginally.

Do you want to learn a new and more effective way of dealing with conflict? Conflict is always emotionally charged and effective conflict management must therefore address both our thinking and our feelings. A holistic approach, which includes the expected and usual cognitive skills but also adds tools from the sciences of behavior and hypnosis, is what is needed!

1

Dr. M. Paula Daoust

My journey with conflict

Years ago, I learned through a painful and career-changing personal experience how critical effective conflict management is in the world of work. I was working as one of six behavior therapists in an organization that served people with developmental disabilities. As a team, we shared ideas, helped each other develop behavior plans for our clients and learned from each other. Since most of us had moved from other parts of the country to work at this organization we were outsiders, in a small town and our work relationships became our social support system as well.

Sherri, my best friend, was a gifted therapist and we spent hours after work talking about our cases and sharing our personal lives with each other. Sherri loved children and didn't have any of her own. She became a special aunt to my boys, attending their athletic and school events and babysitting so that I could have a quiet night with my husband. In return, I would take care of her pets when she went home to visit her parents.

One day, I was called into the superintendent's office and asked whether I would fill in for my direct supervisor who was taking a three month leave of absence. I had never supervised but I was up for the challenge and readily agreed. With no experience or training, I was now managing my friends. What could go wrong?

About two weeks into my new role, while having coffee with Sherri, she complained that the overlap between her role and that of two other therapists had caused confusion in a client's implementation plan. With my new authority, I thought I knew exactly what needed to be done. I quickly worked out a clarification of roles and detailed specific responsibilities for each member of the team. I proceeded to proudly unveil the new plan at the next team meeting.

I was stunned by the push-back and objections. Instead of the chorus of praise I had expected, I got an energetic round of "What?" "Why?" and "NO!" Has anything like that ever happened to you? To make matters worse, Sherri was the most vocal of all in her protest! I felt betrayed – after all, the whole reason I had taken this action was to help her out.

My response was to fall back on my authority as their supervisor and to insist that this was the plan and they would just have to get used to it. I then retreated to my office and found every reason to stay there for days, avoiding all contact with my team. As you would expect, the situation did not settle down. With no opportunity to talk to me, the frustration festered. Because the group felt that they had no other recourse, they took their concerns to the superintendent.

After hearing them out, he could see the problems with the plan and overturned my decision – in retrospect, the plan wasn't really all that good. However, that was probably also not the greatest move on the superintendent's part because I lost credibility and leverage with the team. I served the balance of my time ineffectively hiding in my office and gratefully slipped back into my old role when our supervisor returned to work. But it was not my old job that I returned to, everything had changed. Trust and collegiality with the team had been destroyed and I was alienated from the group. A few months later, I found another job and left the organization.

But all was not lost. I had learned some very important things about myself and about leadership, albeit in a painful way. I had learned just how important good conflict management was for effective leadership. I also became aware of an immense gap in my own development and it became my mission to close that gap.

Good conflict management – more than cognitive tools

I read everything that I could find about conflict management and tried to practice what I had learned. I discovered that conflict management not only involved a specific set of cognitive skills but that it became much more powerful if you can manage your emotions as well. And this requires tools from behavioral science and what I now understand, hypnosis.

All this learning would be called on when I landed my dream job a few years later. I was asked to build a leadership academy for the corporation from the ground up. With a group of critical stakeholders, we developed a list of competencies which future leaders would need if the organization was to be competitive in the market of the future. Managing conflict was obviously high on this list and I began

3

assembling the best possible curriculum and action learning opportunities.

Fifteen years later, and over 20 cohorts of 15 participants each, I can proudly say that by all accounts, the leadership academy accomplished what it set out to do and continues to be tremendously successful. Both qualitative observations and quantitative data indicated that every cohort that has gone through the program had significantly improved their emotional intelligence. If you go to Google Scholar and search on the terms *emotional intelligence* (EQi) and leadership, you will find over five pages of references that correlates EQi and leadership. Assessing participants on their emotional intelligence was a reasonable indicator of leadership development because the research indicates that those individuals with high emotional intelligence are consistently evaluated by others as being leaders.

However, I became aware that the graduates were not using the conflict management skills they had learned. For me, this was an epic fail. What I had observed, repeatedly, was that managers who entered my program struggled with conflict management and, once they had completed the program, they still didn't handle conflict well.

Folks have trouble with difficult conversations, whether it is holding their direct reports accountable or talking to colleagues about sharing resources, collaboration, or their working relationship. Many people avoid these conversations. Or, when they do have them, they hold them poorly and this often makes matters worse. This same issue had derailed my career years earlier and was now threatening to derail these talented managers.

What was frustrating to see was that, during classroom evaluation after the training, these managers could demonstrate that they had mastered the basic skills of holding a healthy, productive conversation. However, the cognitive skills didn't seem to carry over into their real work. When it really mattered, they reverted to avoiding the situation, command and control, or triangulation by appealing to someone, usually their supervisor, to intervene.

After thinking about it for a long time, I realized what the problem was that I was relying too heavily on logical, rational conflict management tools whereas conflict is most often laden with emotions.

Why effective conflict management matters

Both careers and organizations die when conflict festers. If it is not dealt with effectively:

- decisions are made based on incomplete information;
- competition between individuals and departments grow;
- departmental goals are met at the cost of undermining organizational goals;
- talented leaders leave the organization; and,
- over time, the organizational culture becomes increasingly toxic.

This is unacceptable. I want so much more for my organization and I am sure you, too, want better for your organization. At the very least, wouldn't you like to work in a place that helped you to grow and provided you with the kind of working environment that you could look forward to going to, most days?, Do you, like me, want to respect the folks you work with and be respected by them? Would you like to feel confident that when you raise a concern in your organization you can talk through alternatives with others so that today's decisions do not become tomorrow's problems? Would you like to make a difference for yourself, your direct reports, your colleagues, your organization, and for the people your organization serves.

What's stopping you?

I believe that healthy work environments and quality decision-making are possible, but not with our limited approach to conflict management. While cognitive skills help, we must also address the emotional side of conflict if we are really going to make a difference in our outcomes.

Somehow, we need to tame our emotions so that we can use the cognitive skills we have acquired. Without learning how to manage the emotional side of conflict, all our efforts are doomed to mediocre results at best or, more often, to failure. That is the adventure we are about to take; discovering how we can include all parts of the brain, both the emotional and the rational sides, when dealing with conflict.

I'm a little greedy and I hope you are as well! I want to have my cake and eat it too. I want to come through conflict with a good result **and** sustain or enrich my relationship with the other person. In other words, I don't want my outcomes to come at the cost of damaging a relationship that I might need or want in the future. Nor do I want to put all my emphasis on maintaining a relationship while giving up on getting a good outcome.

If you combine the cognitive steps that have already been well documented in the literature, the basic "how to's" of conflict management, with behavioral science and hypnosis, you **can** have your cake and eat it too! You can solve problems in ways that they stay solved and don't become bigger problems tomorrow. You can build your network of support and you can transform adversaries into teammates!

The secret to good conflict management

As a behavioral psychologist and a certified hypnotherapist, I know firsthand that we are not nearly as rational and logical in our actions as we would like to think. Google it and you will find a plethora of articles stating that a mere 5% of our decisions are made with the prefrontal cortex, the seat of our logical, rational thinking. The rest is controlled by our emotional, or limbic, system.

I'm not sure how the experts arrived at this estimate but, with what I know about heuristics, which are our mental decision-making shortcuts, filters and automatic behavior (a.k.a. habits), I am pretty sure that the estimate is not far from the truth. It's no wonder that my graduates were not using the skills they learned in the classroom when faced with a real conflict and all the emotions associated with it. We can do better, much better!

So, what is the secret to successful conflict management? This adventure we are about to start is an adventure worth taking. In the coming chapters we will explore specific tools that will allow you to manage conflict effectively! These tools include both the expected cognitive tools and the less traditional tools from behavioral science and hypnosis. These additional tools, which recruit your emotional brain, will provide you with a powerful, whole-brain approach.

Leaders who effectively resolve conflict and remove barriers, will energize and inspire action. They solve problems and get things done! With improved conflict management skills, you can achieve better health and relationships, and improve your ability to achieve meaningful outcomes. Your work will have greater purpose and you will feel more in control of every aspect of your life. A successful and less stressed work experience is there for the taking!

2

Levels of Conflict

What is conflict?

When you hear the word conflict, what comes to mind? You and I may not mean the same thing when we use this word. That's the problem with any plan for addressing conflict. Since our personal experience and cultural differences can color our understanding of what we mean by conflict, we need to begin with a shared concept.

According to the Merriam Dictionary, conflict is defined as "a competitive or opposing action of incompatibles: antagonistic state or action (as of divergent ideas, interests, or persons)." With this definition, many of the challenges we commonly define as a conflict do not qualify as a conflict. They just do not rise to that level because most of these issues are not "incompatible" or completely "opposing." It might more appropriate to think about conflict as a continuum.

Continuum of conflict

When conflict occurs at any level on the continuum, it triggers our stress response, commonly referred to as the fight-or-flight response. We know we are dealing with some level of conflict because any number of physiological changes occur. These might include an increased heartbeat, shallow and frequent breaths, and sweating. When the level of conflict is minor, these physiological changes are subtle, but they are still present. Long-term exposure to even these subtle changes can cause havoc to both our physical and mental health. Knowing where on the continuum a conflict situation falls is important because not all conflicts need to be addressed with the same approach. Some situations at the lower levels might resolve themselves and can therefore be ignored. Others will need to be addressed, but tools that require less investment of time and emotion can be used. Situations at the higher levels cannot be ignored and, if not handled well, they will usually result in unhappy consequences.

Figure 1: The Conflict Continuum

Beginning with the mildest form of conflict and moving on the most serious, the continuum looks like this:

9

Level 1 – Irritation

Something is amiss; you don't like it but it's not a big deal and you try to let it go. You can do so at first but, as the situation continues and the irritating behavior is repeated, it gets harder and harder to ignore. Eventually, it becomes an earworm, playing and replaying in your head.

Level 2 - Worry or feeling troubled

You are feeling concerned about what is happening or might happen. You don't feel safe and begin to see more and more evidence that, if the situation continues, the future is not going to be good for you.

Level 3 - Misunderstanding

You or the other party failed to understand a set of signals or information and then, took action that is contrary to what was expected or wanted. At the least, this results in disappointment but, more often, the outcome is hurt, resentment and damage to the relationship.

Level 4 - Disagreement

You have a different opinion, or are at variance with someone, about appropriate action. This difference leaves you frustrated and maybe even feeling disrespected by the other person.

Level 5 - Argument

You have developed a strongly held and coherent set of reasons, statements or facts in support of your position and in opposition to another's perspective. An argument is just a disagreement with a lot of added evidence. The evidence is usually one-sided because of our own "confirmation bias," which means we naturally discard or discredit evidence that does not support our position.

At this stage, you are feeling some level of superiority and you may be offended that the other person does not agree with you, given the clear "facts" and reasons which you have provided. You are probably also feeling a level of disrespect for the other person because, in your mind, their position is clearly not as strong as your own. You are now engaging in adversarial thinking. The other person is a rival, the enemy, and a challenger to what you know to be right and this challenge feels like a personal attack.

Level 6 - Dispute

Here a disagreement or argument has escalated to include an emotional element such as anger or frustration. You hold on to your position with persistence because you perceive that the price of losing is too high. At this level, you have dug in. You are convinced that you are right, and the other person is wrong. You are absolutely committed to your perspective and, with raging negative emotions, you don't want to hear any counter arguments or explanations. You are either determined to win or you have resigned yourself to living with an inferior outcome because you just feel too overwhelmed by the uphill battle that would be necessary for the right answer to be implemented. The mental picture of the other person as an adversary is growing. There is a wall between the two of you, making it difficult to see or hear anything from the other side.

Level 7 - Discord

An incompatible set of perspectives. You have slipped into zero-sum thinking; there is only so much pie to go around. Any amount the other person gets means less for you. In this situation, winning is your priority and anything less than total victory is a complete loss. No compromise is possible. To quote an old idiom, "It's my way or the highway!" The other person has graduated to a full-on enemy that must be defeated. Any sense of connection with them has deteriorated and it is now an "us vs. them" world.

You could disagree with the order of the items on this continuum and there could be more levels that should be added, but this should give you the idea that there are different levels of discomfort. As conflict rises through these levels towards discord, it becomes

11

increasingly difficult to resolve and the consequences become increasingly problematic for both parties involved.

Fear and conflict

Even at the lower levels of the conflict continuum, fear presents a serious hurdle to resolving the situation. All conflict is based on a real or perceived threat, and any threat produces fear at the subconscious level. Conflict at any level on the continuum is rooted in the belief that something of value is at risk. For example, you may be worried that addressing the situation will harm the relationship, set you up for retaliation, harm your reputation in some way, or just make matters worse than they already are. When initial attempts at resolving conflict go awry, the degree of perceived threat usually increases.

It doesn't matter what the source of the fear is, the fact that it is present makes it difficult to implement the cognitive, step-by-step set of conflict management skills you may have learned. Fear belongs to the subconscious, emotional brain and most conflict models do little to effectively mitigate fears or to build courage. Relying strictly on the conscious, rational, logical brain to do the hard, risky work of conflict management is a prescription for failure. It's taking a pea shooter to an elephant. It just isn't going to be enough. What is needed to truly control the elephant is a set of more comprehensive tools that integrate the science of behavior and hypnosis.

The rider and the elephant

We are not nearly as rational and logical as we want to believe. As a species, our social environment has advanced dramatically but our brains still have pretty much the same wiring as that of our pre-historic ancestors. Many neuroscientists argue that only 5% of our decisions are made with our pre-frontal cortex, where language, logic and rational thinking resides.

According to this argument, 95% of our decisions are being made by our limbic system and our reptilian brain. The limbic system is where our emotions, habits, and preferences are sourced. The reptilian brain is responsible for basic survival and is both instinctive and impulsive in its effort to protect us from harm. Between our limbic system and our reptilian brain most of our daily decisions are beyond our conscious control!

Jonathan Haidt, in his book, *The Happiness Hypothesis,* provided a great analogy to explain this phenomenon.[1] Imagine a rider and an elephant. The rider is your logical, rational brain - the prefrontal cortex. The rider plans, thinks through problems, and analyzes. Based on this sophisticated mental activity, the rider sets the goal and the direction for the elephant while the elephant provides the power for the journey. Because the rider is on top of the elephant and has the superior brain - after all it is the rider that has language - the rider believes that it is in control!

This arrangement between the rider and the elephant works fine provided that the elephant doesn't disagree with the rider. Think about it – the elephant is probably at least twenty times bigger than the rider! If the elephant gets involved in the decision about what, when or how to proceed, the rider is at the elephant's mercy. The rider can pull, push or plead but unless the elephant is willing, movement in the right direction just doesn't happen. The elephant cannot be controlled through force and this is a frustrating and humbling fact that the rider often denies.

You can describe your effort to manage your elephant in a variety of ways: willpower, determination, self-discipline, resolution, tenacity, perseverance, doggedness, purpose, or firmness. These concepts all depend on force and are therefore powerless against the will of the elephant! You can enter a difficult conversation with the intention to remain calm, and you can promise yourself you won't let your emotions get away from you, but it will all be for naught. Once the elephant is involved, all bets are off!

Typical advice for managing conflict falls apart as soon as our emotions get involved because conflict is inherently an emotional event. Regardless of where the situation we are dealing with falls on the conflict continuum, it involves discomfort and at least some level of fear because something of value is at stake. This is true, even at the simplest level of irritation.

Consider the following example. Your 16-year-old son left his empty glass on the table. You are irritated because you must pick up after him and, adding to your frustration, there is a ring on the table. What is the fear? That your son doesn't respect you and treats you like a servant? That your son doesn't care enough about you to protect your possession, the table? Maybe it's that you fear your son doesn't appreciate all the time, money and effort you have put into providing him with a good life? I could go on and on.

Even in something as minor as a glass left on a table, there is an element of fear. That means that the potential for the elephant to get excited is present through all levels of the conflict continuum and increases as we climb towards discord.

Different conflict management approaches needed for different levels

The tension that accompanies the lower levels on the continuum can be quite healthy and might even help towards creating the kind of discussion that leads to positive outcomes. However, if tension or stress are handled poorly, even at these lower levels, achieving the results you want, or need, could be impossible.

Most of what is referred to as conflict in the business world lies somewhere between the second and sixth levels. Fortunately, conflicts only occasionally rise to the level of discord, which is the most dysfunctional and destructive level. Nevertheless, people tend to refer to all levels along the continuum as conflict. This can cause confusion because, depending on the level, different degrees of effort or even different approaches to managing the conflict may be required.

Most current conflict management models work well with the lower levels of discomfort, but they break down in their ability to resolve conflict at levels six or seven. It's not because these models are wrong, but because, at these highest levels, the conflict now includes a major element of heightened emotionality.

Common models of conflict management depend on cognitive thinking. However, as we have seen, conflict at any level on the continuum of conflict, has an emotional element. Once our emotions are involved, we find it difficult to think rationally and logically. For cognitive skills to be effective, emotionality needs to be turned down. At levels six or seven, and to some extent a case could be made for level five, these models are still useful, but a more comprehensive approach is now needed.

The two case studies discussed in the next chapter clearly illustrate why conflict management needs a comprehensive approach.

Conflict destroys careers

Sharon was a rising star when I met her. She was self-taught, determined and a great example of what you can accomplish if you just don't accept the limitations others place on you. She was a star salesperson, putting up great numbers every quarter and the heir apparent for the job of sales manager. The latter turned out to be her demise and no one saw it coming, especially not her.

Nothing had come easily for Sharon and she had learned how to stand up for herself at a young age. She could curse with the best and wasn't afraid to get aggressive when colleagues got in her way. Sharon was smart and she knew not to lose her temper with a customer but when she got back to the office, her assistant and colleagues were fair game. As long as she was making her numbers, folks looked the other way. Eventually, however, this pattern of behavior caught up with her.

Sharon was promoted when the sales manager job finally became available. It didn't take long for morale to shift downwards and, with it, the sales numbers slipped. Sharon's go-to response was to threaten, curse, and demean her staff. If you asked her, she would say they needed someone to light a fire under them.

What was so interesting was that Sharon cared deeply for the people who worked for her. When Allen's daughter broke her arm, Sharon brought her a giant teddy bear and when Martha's mom was ill, Sharon insisted she take time off to be with her. Sharon's kindness was so out of step with her tyrannical drive for performance, that it left her team confused. Ryan told me, "I want to trust her, there are moments when I really like her, but most of the time, I just avoid her." Others weren't quite so generous in describing their relationship with Sharon.

One day, things came to a head when Jamal lost an important sale and Sharon publicly berated and demeaned him during a staff meeting. Several members of Sharon's team made a formal complaint to HR.

She was given a warning and was required to work with an executive coach. She showed improvement for a short while but eventually slipped back into her old behavior patterns. In the end, Sharon was dismissed. Such a waste of tremendous talent!

Another example is Dayton. He wasn't getting along with his supervisor, Luis. Dayton made what he thought was an essential procedural change to accommodate the volatile external reality of a fast-changing competitive environment. Dayton felt undermined and handcuffed when Luis overturned his changes. His response was to write a five-page, detailed report explaining why the change was essential and the potential negative consequences of Luis' decision.

Dayton sent the report to Luis, of course, but he also sent it to several other team members who were affected by the decision. He told me that he did this in hope that others would step up and support him. The report didn't go over well with Luis. When I questioned Luis about the situation he said, "I don't know who Dayton thinks he is. I've been doing this job for 10 years and I don't need an upstart telling me what I should and shouldn't do. And I sure didn't appreciate his involving others! That kind of insubordination is unacceptable." With this perspective, it was not surprising that he put Dayton on a discipline plan. Shocked by Luis' response, Dayton resigned two weeks later. Once again, such a waste of talent. Further, Dayton probably didn't even understand how he had created his own demise.

I am sure you have your own stories of very talented people getting in their own way. Hopefully that person was not you!

Consequences of poor conflict management

All parties involved pay a major price when conflict is not handled well, including the organization. Sharon knew how to sell better than anyone else in the organization but her go-to style when any of her direct reports' performances disappointed her was not to guide and teach them, but rather to punish them. Her first assumption was that their failure was a motivational issue when for most of them, it was skills that were missing. They could have learned so much from Sharon but that didn't happen. Instead, they learned to avoid her at all costs. Unfortunately, you cannot punish someone out of a skill gap and the more she gave in to her temper, the worse their performance became.

Sharon lost her job, her sales team lost an opportunity to learn from a master, and the organization suffered the consequences of tanking sales.

Instead of approaching Luis directly, Dayton resorted to keyboard courage. The price was that Luis felt disrespected and could not give Dayton's concerns fair consideration. Dayton found himself looking for work and Luis lost a direct report that cared deeply about the company. Furthermore, the organization suffered the consequences of not dealing with an external threat.

What difference does it make if a leader is or isn't good at managing conflict? Talk to the former leaders of companies like Toys R Us, Borders, Compaq, Kodak, Xerox, Sears, J.C. Penney, Blockbuster, Nordstroms, and on and on and on. Bad things happen when leaders do not have deep conversations in which they are able to consider multiple scenarios, disagree respectfully, and learn from each other. Decisions are based on incomplete or wrong information. Internal competition grows and the culture of the organization becomes increasingly unsafe. When people feel unsafe, their thinking becomes focused on immediate survival, they look for the choice that is safest in the short-run and the quality of their problem-solving deteriorates.

Clearly, chronic, unmitigated conflict is not good for an organization but what about you? What are the consequences for you if you are not good at managing conflict? Unmitigated conflict produces stress, you don't have to be a rocket scientist to know that. Information about the negative impact of chronic stress on our health is growing by the day. It also has a very big impact on your career. When you are stressed, you are not at your best. Your thinking is not as clear, and you miss seeing answers that may be right in front of you.

In contrast, people who are good at solving problems get promoted. It's that simple. Your career is going to move forward if you can resolve conflict in such a way that you arrive at good outcomes while also creating a stronger network of colleagues that trust you and therefore support you. Even if you don't get a promotion (which you will), going to work each day will be more fun and the stress you feel at work will be eustress (yes, that is a word) and not distress. Eustress leaves you feeling happy, accomplished and in control. It increases your sense of wellbeing and, while at the end of the day you may feel physically tired, you will also feel energized by your work.

Neither you nor your organization can afford to handle any level of conflict poorly. The consequences are too high. On a more positive side, when you do handle conflict well, you get a reputation for being able to get things done and, more importantly, you are personally less stressed, and work is more fun. If the price for not handling it well is so high and the bonus so high when it is done well, it seems like a no-brainer, everyone should place a priority on learning how to handle conflict well! But that is not what you see in the business world. You don't have to look far to see very smart people getting in their own way. Why? Because handling conflict is hard when we insist on doing so with only our rational, logical brain!

3

Dealing with Conflict: Common Approaches

Two standard responses to conflict

Without conscious application of conflict management strategies, people's usual responses to conflict fall on a continuum between two clubs: the Valiant Warrior Club and the White Knight Club. Our responses in either of these two clubs are mostly dysfunctional.

Members of the Valiant Warrior Club see the conflict as a battlefield, and they enter with the intent to conquer it. The Valiant Warrior wants to win because they feel righteous about their pursuit. They are the victim because they have been wronged by the other party. They deserve to win, and the other party deserves to be punished. They are playing a zero-sum game. Any part of the pie the other party gets means less for them. They want a complete admission of wrongdoing from the other party: "I was wrong and you are absolutely right." They also want the other party to concede to all their demands and promise reparation. These are the folks Dr. Phil calls "right-fighters."

Members of the White Knight Club either discount the future and sit idly by or they marshal forces through triangulation. In either case, they are waiting for the White Knight to come by and rescue them. They are innocent victims and need someone else to fight the battle for them.

The first type of member in this club is the helpless victim. They believe that there is nothing they can do to change the situation and so they sit idly by, allowing the situation to continue. They tell themselves it's not really happening, it's not that bad, they can wait it out, they aren't going to let it bother them, and so forth. They discount the future in order to justify their continued inaction. Discounting the future firstly involves over-estimating the consequences of acting now. Secondly, the consequences of not acting are under-estimated. They emphasize the present danger and they discount the degree of danger that inaction will cause in the future.

The other type of in the White Knight Club member is the triangulator. Triangulating in a conflict means that a third (or more) party is brought into the conflict. The conflict is no longer between two parties but rather between two sides. The triangulator marshals allies in their defense. They might recruit colleagues to their cause, arguing that, "everyone feels the way I do." Alternatively, they plead their case to people with more power or authority.

A person can often bounce between the Valiant Warrior and the White Knight clubs. They might start off by trying to be the Valiant Warrior and then, when they don't like the results, they swing over to the White Knight Club. When that isn't working either, they might swing back to their original position. These swings can happen quickly and frequently.

The result of membership to either club is the same, the conflict increases in intensity and dysfunction. The battle is never won, and the White Knight never comes. If you are like me, you don't want to believe that you are ever a member of either club. It's interesting that when I am in a conflict, I don't see myself as being at war or waiting for a White Knight. I just see the conflict and I am holding on tight to the story I have told myself.

It's easy to slip into either/or thinking. We do it all the time. Do you want to go to a movie or out to dinner? Why not both or maybe something else entirely? Watch how often you ask yourself or someone else an either/or question when there are really many, many alternatives. The consequences of either/or thinking are minor when we are deciding how to spend an evening. They have very big consequences, however, when we are responding to a tense situation.

The outcomes of either going to war or waiting to be rescued are not good. But if they are the only options available, we settle for one or the other and get more of what we already have and don't want. If I go to war, the other party is going to defend themselves and the situation is going to become more intense and destructive for everyone involved. The result – more tension, anger, frustration, suspicion, and other negative consequences. We get more of what we already had and didn't want! If we go the other way and wait to be rescued, the other party continues their pattern of behavior, and our resentment grows. This causes havoc to our emotional and physical health. Again, we get more of what we already have and don't want!

Thomas and Kilmann Model of conflict management

What we need is a healthier response to dealing with conflict. Membership in either the Valiant Warrior Club or the White Knight Club is not working. Probably the most sited conflict management model is Thomas and Kilmann's (1974) five conflict management styles.[2] This model argues that there are five distinct approaches to dealing with conflict and these five styles of conflict resolution can be organized on two continuums: concern for others and concern for self.

Figure 2: Thomas and Kilmann's Conflict Model

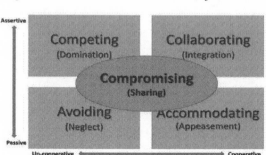

Withdraw: Avoiding or withdrawing from a conflict demonstrates a lack of courage and is low on both concerns for others and for self. People who use this style generally feel a lack of confidence or they simply don't care about the outcome.

Contest: This involves standing your ground and with this style, the focus is on the self. You are competing with the other person(s) and winning is the priority. This style creates resentment and can spiral into open hostility if the other party also contests.

Concede: Giving in involves accommodating the other party and letting them have their way. It is usually based on feeling intimidated or just a deep distaste for conflict. A person using this style will find themselves feeling resentful and self-esteem is eroded as others take advantage of them. Conceding usually leads to further conflict.

Compromise: When this style is used, both parties give a little but neither party gets what they truly want or may need. Although "fair," compromise is rarely ideal because the outcome is seldom the best possible outcome.

Collaborate: This style takes the most effort because it emphasizes the needs of both parties. Outcomes are a balance of needs, neither party satisfying their needs at the expense of the other. It often takes creativity and deep discussion to arrive at an outcome that both parties can live with and feel that they are satisfied.

The Thomas and Kilmann model is a good description of the territory but it is problematic in two ways.

First, it is a description of approaches but without much information about how to execute. Since, according to this model, the collaborative style is the only truly productive approach, its major contribution is that it allows you to diagnose which style is being used. With this knowledge, you can then understand why you may not be getting what you need or want when you attempt to deal with a conflict.

The second issue with this model is that it is based on the premise that we can choose which style we will use when faced with a conflict. I don't know if it happens to you, but when dealing with a difficult conversation, my intentions don't last very long. I might enter with the intention of being collaborative but when things get tense, I find myself withdrawing or contesting. Does this happen to you? You set out to take the high ground and quickly find yourself engaging in less than admirable behavior? Intentions and actual behavior are often two different things, and this is one of the reasons why conflict management is so difficult.

Other models of conflict management

If you Google *conflict management*, you will arrive at a plethora of sites offering tips or a more detailed set of steps for dealing with conflict. The more systematic models usually include some version of the following steps.

- Get clear on exactly what the issue is. If you aren't clear within yourself, you won't be clear with the other party.
- Share your concern or issue with the other party, including how it is impacting you. Be careful to present this information in a non-judgmental and calm way.
- Listen to the other person's perspective and try to understand the issue from their vantage point.
- Based on a common understanding of the issue, negotiate an outcome that is agreeable to both parties.

This is an oversimplification of many very good approaches to conflict management. Different authors have added other nuances to their models. A list of the twenty most common tips for conflict management is available for download at https://conflictatworkbook.com/resources/.

The problem with the standard steps for managing conflict is that this approach suffers from the same issues that reduce the usefulness of the Thomas and Kilmann model. They assume that conflict can be managed with rational steps and that we can control our emotions, if we choose to do so. I wish that this were true, and I am sure you do, too. In my experience, when I am dealing with conflict, my best intentions to remain logical and rational quickly slip away. In those moments, words come out of my mouth that my mother would not be proud of and which I regret almost as quickly as I have said them. Or, almost as bad, I don't think to say the things I should have said and needed to say.

23

A more comprehensive model

There is one conflict model that recognizes the emotional aspect of conflict management and offers some tools for guiding the elephant. I am a big fan of the book *"Crucial Conversations"* by Patterson, Grenny, McMillan, and Switzler.[3] According to the authors, people don't resist you because they don't care about you. They resist you because they believe you don't care about them or what they care about. That is another way of saying that people are afraid that you don't have their best interests at heart.

People fear that unless they take action to protect themselves, you will do them harm. Earlier, I stated that a sense of threat is at the root of all conflict. There is the fear that something of value is being threatened. If I don't believe you care about me, then the corollary is that your needs, wants, and priorities are more important to you than mine. I expect that you are looking out for yourself and that puts me at odds with you. Essentially, we are on opposite sides of a wall.

Crucial Conversations is different from other models because it recognizes that a conflict is rarely about what actually happened but, more often, about the meaning people attach to the event. The authors describe this as the story people tell themselves about what happened.

Meaning-making and conflict

As a species, we are meaning-makers or storytellers. It's one of the things that separates us from all other species. I love my dog and sometimes I almost believe she is human. But one thing I know for sure is that when I tell my fur baby, "Wait!" she isn't wondering if I don't love her anymore, or if I think that I'm more important than her, or, whether I don't think that her needs or wants matter. She doesn't attach meaning or a story to my command. The only thing that my fur baby knows is that, whatever it is she wants, she isn't going to get it right now!

It's just the opposite if I tell my husband to wait. All kinds of things are going through his mind and depending on the situation, he might take exception to being told to wait or he might respond with great patience. The meaning he attaches to my telling him to wait will depend on the context and what other information is available. In a split second he will make an assumption about my intention and that becomes the story he tells himself. My husband has added meaning to the simple word, "wait." He cannot read my mind and, unless there is a lot of information indicating that it is quite appropriate to wait, he is probably going to tell himself a negative story about my intention. He might tell himself that, in the moment, I am not respecting him, or am trying to control him, or maybe that I am treating him like a child. He can't read my mind (fortunately!). If he could, he might have understood that I just wanted to share something with him, or, that I had a surprise which I didn't want him to spoil. There could have been any number of other reasons for asking him to wait, all of them more positive than the negative story about my intentions which he came up with.

Imagine that you sent Jan, a colleague, an email at the end of the day asking for help with something before the meeting you were both attending the next day at 9 a.m. When you got to work early the next day, you were greeted with an email from Jan saying, "I don't have time for this right now." What possible meaning might you attach to this simple response? What do you think Jan's intentions are? What story are you telling yourself about Jan's email to you?

You could easily come up with several stories, but chances are that your first assumptions about Jan's intentions were not generous! You might have thought, "She doesn't care about what I need," or, "She doesn't want to help me," or "She is so competitive, she won't help me because then I might look better than her at the meeting." The list of stories you could tell yourself is endless, and most of them are not very nice stories about Jan's intentions. But maybe, just maybe, it occurred to you that Jan is feeling a lot of pressure right now and that she didn't mean to come across as so abrupt. That's a much nicer, more empathetic story!

Half an hour later, you see Jan rushing past your desk and she doesn't respond when you say hello. What are you thinking now? Has your assumption about Jan's email response gotten even darker? Are you even more convinced that Jan isn't being very nice to you? If you had been generous and thought that maybe Jan was feeling a lot of pressure, how generous are you feeling now? Are you doubting that empathetic story?

25

Now it's 9 a.m. and you arrive at the meeting. Jan is passing out papers and when she passes the papers to you, they skid across the table. What are you thinking now? Are you feeling any empathy for the pressure Jan is under? Or is there a growing suspicion that something ugly is going on between you and Jan? Are those ugly, negative stories growing? By now, your story about Jan is probably that she is the "enemy." Your fight-or-flight response has probably been fully ignited because your brain has taken in several examples of Jan's behavior and attached meaning to them. You are now telling yourself a story that Jan is a threat, that she means you harm, or at the very least, does not intend to be helpful to you.

How do you respond? You are probably not going to be very supportive of anything she has to say in the meeting, and you might even be openly critical! The worst is that you will often respond in this way without even thinking about it – you aren't deliberately being difficult with Jan, but the story about her intentions towards you are subconsciously coloring everything you hear and see. You are continuing to attach meaning to everything and your story is distinctly *dark and getting darker!*

Scenarios like this happen all day, every day. Things happen, and at lightning speed we attach meaning to these events. We tell ourselves a story about other people's intentions. Sometimes, the meaning we attach is correct. However, because we are biased by our drive for self-preservation to see threat, we usually attach the wrong meaning. When this happens, we can and do respond with aggression, protection or avoidance when there really is no threat present.

Telling ourselves not to attach meaning to events is a waste of energy because it happens so quickly, that we don't even realize that we have done it. That complicates the issue. Because it happens so fast, we easily confuse the meaning which we attach to an event with the actual event itself. This very close pairing between an event and attaching a meaning to it marries the two - they become one - and this merging becomes our truth! This can cause havoc to our relationships because we are walking around defending ourselves or avoiding others based on a fiction we have devised for ourselves. If this isn't bad enough, the very act of defending ourselves or avoiding a situation or person provides them with information that colors their experience with us.

They begin responding to our behavior with aggression, protection or avoidance, and this creates a downward spiral!

Let's see how this works in your relationship with Jan. You have become convinced that Jan is not your ally and may even be intending to cause you harm. You become abrupt with her, you avoid her, and you are even critical of her work. In a very short period, she senses this antagonistic distance and she begins to feel that you are not her ally and may even do her harm. Even if her behavior was originally innocent, it has now slipped into something else because she now believes that you are not a friend. As a result, her behavior towards you changes and she becomes defensive or openly antagonistic. Now you have additional information that she should not be trusted. Can you see how this can turn and turn and turn?

Facts vs. meanings

Does this imply that we are victims of our meaning-making? Certainly not. We are not doomed to the downward spiral. At any given point, we have a choice. We can challenge the meaning we have attached to an event or we can accept it. That analytical, thinking brain of ours can step back and ask, "Is it real or am I attaching the wrong meaning?"

The problem is that we are very fond of our meanings and we don't like giving them up. Because they happen so fast, they get confused with the facts and they feel like the truth. To even suggest that they might not be factual but rather the meaning we attached to the facts, feels wrong.

Television personality, Dr. Phil McGraw, is fond of asking a question that is worth considering here, "How is that working out for you?" If the meaning you have attached to an event is contributing to a better relationship with people in your life and you are getting the results you want, while also strengthening your relationships, then you don't need to read any further. More likely, however, is that you are either getting results at the cost of important relationships, or you are maintaining relationships at the cost of getting the results you need. If so, it's time to consider re-thinking the meaning you have attached to events!

The key to managing a difficult situation is to separate what really happened from the story you have told yourself. In other words, you need to change the meaning of the event. When we do that, we naturally change how we feel about the event.

Take for example the following situation. Tonia, your 14-year-old daughter, had a day off from school but you had to go to work. You asked her if she would get supper started by peeling the potatoes and getting some meat out of the freezer to defrost. Not an unreasonable set of requests. You get home and neither task was completed. You are frustrated because supper will now be much later. The meaning you attach to the undone chores is that Tonia just doesn't take her responsibilities seriously.

Tonia comes into the house from the backyard and you immediately begin to righteously express your disappointment and frustration. After a couple of minutes of this, Tonia interrupts. She explains that the neighbor's 7-year-old fell and hurt her arm. Tonia volunteered to help by watching the other toddlers so that the child's mom could get the 7-year-old some medical attention. Oops!! It appears that your daughter was anything but irresponsible! In a matter of seconds you moved from angry, frustrated, and disappointed to impressed, proud and probably, a little embarrassed. When the meaning changed, so did your feelings and in this case, the conflict disappeared.

Two very different meanings could be attached to the same set of facts. The meaning you attached was based on past experience with Tonia and was quite plausible. Despite this, it was wrong! In this scenario, Tonia quickly offered the additional fact that she was helping the neighbor. This gave you an easy and obvious opportunity to adjust your meaning. The problem comes when we are convinced our meaning is right and we act on it as if the meaning were a fact.

Three steps to taking control

If there is a relationship in your life that could and should be improved (and I don't know of anyone who can honestly say that all their relationships are hunky-dory) then it's time to take control of your meanings. Here is how you do it.

First, you will need to recognize that for every event, there can be many stories that fit the same set of facts.

Let me give you an example. A friend, Hannah, accepted a position as a manager with a new employer. As it happened, Sally, one of her new direct reports, had also applied for the position and obviously, did not get it. Sally had worked in the department for over six years and was quite vocal about her disappointment about not being promoted. She even openly questioned Hannah's qualifications. Although their relationship didn't start well, they both worked on it.

Three months into the new position, Hannah decided to make an important change in a critical process. Before doing so, she ran the decision past Sally who expressed no concerns about the change. Hannah was called into her supervisor's office a week later and was reprimanded for making the change. It turned out that Hannah's decision ran contrary to an unwritten rule and it caused problems for other areas in the department.

When Hannah came to me, she said,

"Sally is sabotaging me. She didn't get the position and now she is setting me up. She knew what was going to happen when we made that change and she didn't warn me!"

I asked Hannah what other explanations might fit the same set of facts. At first Hannah's response was predictable. She defended the story she had told me about Sally's intentions. I pushed her to just play with the idea that there could be other stories that fit the same set of facts. What were the facts?

- Sally wanted the manager's position;
- Sally had worked in the department for several years;
- Sally knew Hannah was going to make a change;
- Sally knew the change would affect other areas of the company; and,
- Sally didn't warn Hannah.

I asked Hannah for five other stories that would fit these five facts. After she thought about it, she provided the following alternative stories:

1. Maybe Sally didn't like the process and was happy that it was finally being changed.

2. Sally might have thought that I had already gotten permission to make the change.

3. Maybe Sally thought that the other areas were aware of the change and were adjusting.

4. Sally might have been afraid that I would be upset with her if she questioned my decision.

5. Sally might have thought there was no point in questioning the decision because I wouldn't listen to her perspective anyway.

One could probably come up with another ten or more stories that would fit the same set of facts. Hannah's story might have been the truth, but so could any of the others. By the way, just because it's a story doesn't mean it isn't true! So how would Hannah know the true story? She will never know the real story if she doesn't recognize that her story is only one of many possible stories! It means that Hannah must let go of her conviction that her story **is** right.

This brings us to the **second** thing needed to effectively manage conflict. To get better results and simultaneously deepen important relationships means that you will want to consider what other meanings will fit the same facts. To do this, you need to notice that you have attached a meaning to the facts! This level of self-awareness is not common or easy. As discussed earlier, the meaning and the facts happen so close together that we tend to see them as one and the same. To quote Dr. Phil again, "Do you want to be a right fighter?" or do you want a better result?

Note that I keep saying a better result, not your result. This distinction is very important. If you are determined to get a specific result, you will not be open to hearing another meaning or even considering that there might be another meaning for the same set of facts. When you are focused on a specific result, your filters will dismiss anything that does not fit your belief that you have the right to the result you expect. A better result means that you get a result that supports the needs and wants of both parties. It isn't a compromise. It is truly a good result for both sides. The only way you can get a better result is to be open to considering that your meaning may not be the only or the true meaning.

The **third** thing necessary for getting a better result and nurturing important relationships brings us to an earlier point, separating the facts from your meaning. They get merged so quickly it sometimes takes practice to be able to pull them apart. What is a fact and what is a story?

A fact is something that happened. If two or more people had been in the room, all would agree that it occurred. A fact is objective. It can be seen, heard, felt, or measured. In contrast, a meaning is a conclusion, judgment, or an attribution. Just to be clear, an attribution is any quality or feature that is characteristic of, or possessed by, a person or thing.

In the following examples, the facts are separated from conclusions, judgments and attributions.

- *He stomped into the room angrily*:

  Fact: He entered the room.

  Meaning: "*Stomped*" is a judgment about the way he entered the room and "*angrily*" is an attribution about an emotion he possessed.

- *She was thrilled with her gift and thanked me profusely*:

  Fact: She thanked me for her gift.

  Meaning: "*Thrilled*" is an attribution about her emotion and "*profusely*" is a judgment about the degree of thanks she offered.

- *He is always late; he's lazy and just isn't that motivated*:

  Fact: He is late and if records are checked, he has probably been late often.

  Meaning: "*Always*" is a judgment, "*lazy*" is an attribution and "*he just isn't that motivated*" is a conclusion.

Recognizing a meaning

When trying to separate facts from meanings, consider that absolutes are usually stories because there is rarely a mechanism for objectively assessing them as facts. Absolutes include words such as: all, none, must, except, every, not, always, just, only, and never. If I say, "you never take out the trash," you might point out that on January 14, 2017, you did take out the trash! Never is a very big word and there is a good chance that there is an exception somewhere in a person's history. The same issue is present with the other absolute terms.

Another thing to watch for are adjectives and adverbs. These two parts of speech are good indicators, although not always, that there might be a story embedded in your statement. Adjectives and adverbs are descriptive words that add color to an account. By its very nature, a description is a representation of something, and two people can easily provide different representations of the same event.

Have you ever attended a presentation or listened to a speech with a friend and when you discussed it afterwards, it felt as though the two of you did not attend the same event? You each filtered the content according to your own values and beliefs and had very different interpretations about what was said. You added your own meaning to the words you heard and, as a result, you had a different story about what happened! Adjectives and adverbs are part of the meaning you attach to events around you and another observer is quite likely to choose different adverbs or adjectives.

Attributions are particularly tricky. An attribution is any quality or feature that is characteristic of, or possessed by, a person or thing. We love attributions because they are shortcuts. If I say, "The girl is happy," I believe that I have communicated a significant piece of information about the girl's affect with one word. The problem is that attributions are shortcuts, or, as I like to think of them, code words. A code word is any word that is translated in our heads. Happy can mean a lot of different things, depending on the context and your own particular history. The word "mad" can be translated in your head to many other code words, like "angry" or "mentally unstable." In other words, a code word is a representation of several possible behaviors. I might say, "She is happy," because I see her smiling and clapping her hands or maybe because she said, "This is wonderful."

Code words are based on one or more observed behaviors and they provide a quick way of summarizing these behaviors. We love code words because they are efficient. We choose our code word based on observed behavior, but then the listener quickly merges the word with other possible behaviors and believes that they have understood your message. When I say she is happy, and I am referring to her smile, you may be translating "happy" to a set of different behaviors such as bouncing and laughing. Code words are imprecise and seductive because they trick us into believing we have communicated information accurately. However, there is no way to know for sure how the listener interpreted the word. Worse yet, the listener assumes that they accurately understood what you communicated!

The lesson here is that, for better results, we must get better at recognizing when we have attached a meaning so that we can challenge it. Remember, just because it is a story doesn't mean it isn't true. However, when we can recognize that we have attached our own meaning, we become open to hearing other versions.

Frequently, the meaning we have attached is only partly true. For example, "Allen is always late because he is lazy and unmotivated." If we challenge our meaning, the attributions "lazy and unmotivated," we can recognize that he did, in fact, arrive late. If we check his work sign-in sheet, we also discover that he has been late several times in the last couple of weeks. And yes, when we check with Allen, we discover that while he would have preferred to be on time, he was more motivated to address some competing demands. One of his instances of tardiness was because he had to find daycare for a sick child at the last minute. Another tardy was because he needed to find alternative transportation when his car wouldn't start. In each tardy Allen was working hard to resolve a pressing issue and, given his challenges, he did get to work fairly quickly. Your story wasn't completely wrong, it's just that there was more to the story and you didn't have access to the rest of the story until you checked it out!

Returning to Jan and her abrupt behavior towards you (yes, abrupt is a description and therefore a story – you're getting good at this!), What were the facts in Jan's situation?

- You asked Jan for help in an email at the end of a working day.
- Jan answered with a one sentence response that she couldn't help you.

- Jan walked past your desk at a quick pace and did not return your greeting.
- Jan handed out papers at the meeting and the ones intended for you were pushed in your direction and not given to you directly.

For something to be a fact, two observers would agree on the same statements about an event or series of events. If someone else had been present, could that person verify each of the above statements? Absolutely.

Ask Jan for her version of each of the facts and we would have the rest of the story. First, she got the email when she was on her way out the door and so she responded quickly, "I don't have time for this right now." The next day, she was in a hurry to get her report copied. While rushing to the photocopier, she didn't see you sitting at your desk, much less hear your greeting. Jan got to the meeting and was trying to get the reports distributed quickly before your supervisor arrived. You were at the end of the table and it would have taken a little more energy to get the papers to you and she didn't have time to walk to your side of the room because she could hear your supervisor in the hall.

Now, how do you feel about the series of events? Have your feelings about Jan changed? Are you as suspicious about her intention towards you? Your story about Jan has probably changed and it might now include code words like disorganized, stressed, or maybe even, procrastinator!

The fallacy of seeing conflict as an either/or situation allows us to rationalize counterproductive behavior. In Chapter 2 we saw Sharon argue that she had to go to war. She was a member of the Valiant Warrior Club and believed going to war was for the good of the organization and for her subordinates' own good. She couldn't just sit back and let them continue with sub-standard performance. She had to light a fire under them! It was her responsibility. Dayton didn't have the power to go to war directly with his supervisor. He believed that to have openly challenged Luis would certainly be grounds for dismissal. Instead, he went the White Knight Club route and attempted to rally support from his colleagues. From his perspective, it was his only option.

In search of a better way

Neither Sharon nor Dayton achieved what they had set out to do. Sharon didn't get better performance from her staff and Dayton didn't sway his supervisor to accept the changes he wanted. But both Sharon and Dayton would argue they played the only card they had because the cost of the other card was just too high.

When we give in to the either/or fallacy, we oversimplify our options and blind ourselves to the real opportunities. For both Sharon and Dayton, there were other options. Sharon didn't need to attack her staff, nor did she have to accept poor performance. She could have worked on understanding the challenges from their perspective and helped them grow in their skills. Dayton didn't have to resort to triangulating to put pressure on Luis, nor did he need to challenge him. He could have talked the situation through and he might have better understood why Luis felt the need to overturn his decision. Adding to this either/or thinking is the problem of miscommunicating through the use of code words and the meanings we attach to those word, and it's no wonder that conflict is so difficult to manage.

Something is still missing

According to Maya Angelou, "When you know better, do better!" but that doesn't always happen. In the case of conflict, it just isn't that easy! It is anything but easy when we are restricted to managing the conflict situations with only our conscious, rational brain. The belief that handling conflict can be done this way is a waste to organizations that must shoulder the cost of poor decisions, damaged performance and expensive turnover. It is a major waste for individuals whose careers become derailed. It isn't necessary and it can be different.

Are you setting yourself up for poorer performance, bad decisions, or derailment because you are trying to handle conflict poorly? Using your whole brain, both your rational, logical brain and your emotional brain, will make all the difference!

I have been coaching individual contributors, supervisors, managers, directors and even C-Suite folks to manage conflict for over 10 years. In the classroom and in a one-to-one coaching situation, they correctly demonstrate the skills in role-plays. They know how to implement a five-step model, separate facts from their meaning and challenge either/or thinking, but I still didn't see many of these folks using these skills in a real situation. It was a major disappointment and frustration because I believed that if they did use these skills, they would get the results they needed and build stronger relationships.

So, what was the problem? I have thought about this a lot and I have come to believe that the issue goes back to fear. Something happens and the meaning which we attach to the situation is that we are in danger. Our elephant is fully engaged. Telling ourselves that we are not in danger is not enough to calm our elephant. Our emotions are blocking our ability to even begin using any of the conflict management skills that we have learned, and we resort to our old patterns of self-protection.

Unless we can recruit our emotions towards positive change at the outset, we will do one of two things:

- Hold on to our meaning that the other person has wronged us and is therefore responsible for correcting the situation by changing their behavior. This gives us the right to become a Valiant Warrior; or

- Rationalize why we can't, shouldn't or don't need to have the difficult conversation. We stand by, waiting for our White Knight to arrive and rescue us.

In either case, the outcome is going to be exactly what we don't want. We will either give up on getting the result we want and feel further victimized or we will get what we want by making demands and risk damaging the relationship.

There is an alternative

We can use the PPE model of conflict management. The commonly recognized meaning of the acronym PPE is Personal Protective Equipment. I believe that is exactly what we need to manage conflict. We need the equipment to feel protected and safe so that we can have the courage to use the cognitive tools that have been shown to work.

In the context of this book, PPE stands for Prepare your emotions; Plan your conversation; and Execute your plan. While the model is represented as a linear process, it is really just a way of organizing many tools, some of which usually happen early in the sequence and some later. All the tools could be used at any time before, during or even after the difficult conversation.

In the following chapters we will explore using this model to engage the whole brain when managing conflict.

Preparing Your Emotions

The next two chapters are focused on getting your mind in the right place for having a difficult conversation with someone. First, you need to understand what exactly is happening in your body as you anticipate conflict and when you are in the midst of conflict. Second, you have to change your mindset towards focusing on positivity or the conversation is almost guaranteed to go askew.

Without preparing your emotions, you may get a result, but it might be at the cost of damaging an important relationship. Or, to avoid angering or hurting the other party, you might talk yourself out of addressing the issue or you might just soft-sell the issue. You can get both, a good outcome AND nurture the relationship as well, but it has to start with preparing your emotions.

4

Conflict and Your Body

Wired for the dark side

Imagine that you and some friends had been planning a camping trip for several months. After several long discussions and much negotiation, the group decided the Black Hills of South Dakota would be the perfect destination. Your group planned who would bring which camping gear and food. In the following weeks you shopped for all the food and necessary supplies. The day finally came, and the cars were packed. At 5 a.m. you began the long eleven-hour drive from Topeka to the campground. With a few stops along the way, the caravan of three cars arrived at the gates of the park at 6 p.m. Tired and anxious to get settled, you met with the park ranger to register for your camping spots. The ranger was warm and friendly, but you could feel that something wasn't quite right. After filling out the usual forms and before you actually paid your fees, the ranger says,

"There's something you should know. We don't have a lot of campers right now because, in the last couple of weeks, we have had a couple of incidents with bears looking for food. If you still want to camp, I have a list of things you need to do to keep your food secure. If you follow these guidelines, the bears shouldn't bother you."

Hotels aren't easy to find in the Black Hills and you and your friends had driven a long way. After talking it over, the group decided they could follow the guidelines and wanted to go ahead and set up camp. You paid the fees and headed into the park. On the bright side, with fewer campers, you were able to find a truly picturesque location, wooded trees all around your camping spot and a stream just a couple of hundred feet from where you intended to pitch your tents. It was perfect.

A couple of hours later, with tents all set up and supper over, you and your friends are sitting around the campfire and enjoying an adult beverage, coffee or tea, of course! Suddenly, in the brush just beyond the light of the campfire, you hear a crash and sense something moving closer and closer. Without a second thought, you are on your feet looking for something with which to protect yourself and assessing the distance between you and your car. Just before you take off running, a big fat raccoon steps into the light and then, just as fast as it had appeared, it scurries back into the darkness and off into the brush. You realize now that the sound you heard was the raccoon. Everyone sits back down, laughing and poking fun at each other. What a great story!

Here is an important question. What did it cost you to assume that the unexpected change was dangerous when in fact it was not? Nothing besides a few calories, right? But let's assume that, instead of jumping to your feet and preparing to run or to fight, you remained relaxed and told your friends everything was fine. Then, out of the brush and into the fire light stepped a big, black bear? Now what would it have cost you to assume that the change was safe when in fact it was quite dangerous? Right, it could cost you your life!

Survival means that we are wired for the dark side! When something happens, and we don't have all the details it is safer to assume that the "something" will cause us harm. If we do so, we can use precious seconds to prepare ourselves!

Loss aversion

To make matters a little more complicated, behavioral economics has demonstrated that we are more motivated to avoid a loss than to acquire a similar gain. What that means is that we are wired to protect what we already have.

Carlos, a real estate agent, deals with this all the time. When he recommends a selling price to a potential seller, they usually argue that it's not enough and want to start at a higher price. When shopping for their next home, however, they almost always feel that the seller has priced their home too high. Without consciously being aware of it, they have overvalued their own possession and undervalued that of another. They are also highly motivated to keep as much of their own money as possible by insisting on the bottom price for the house they are purchasing. At the same time, they are expecting others to give them top price for their home because, after all, it is worth it, and they aren't going to "give it away".

Besides loss aversion, we need to add another behavioral economics principle, the endowment effect. This principle states that ownership creates satisfaction. These two principles working together means that we are going to work hard to keep what we already have because it brings us great satisfaction to own it. This satisfaction increases its value to us. We aren't going to let it go without a fair exchange and our version of the fair exchange is magnified by the satisfaction it brings us. Since we overvalue our own possessions and undervalue those of others, it is very difficult to achieve a fair exchange because others are using the same skewed math while negotiating with us. It is amazing that compromises ever happen!

Three brains in one

Functionally, we have three brains, the reptilian brain, the limbic system and the prefrontal cortex. These three parts work together closely, but we are usually unaware of their synchrony.

The reptilian brain

The most primitive brain is often referred to as the *reptilian brain* because our version of this part of the brain is pretty much the same as that of a reptile. It is instinctive, acts unconsciously and is concerned

41

with survival. From an evolutionary perspective, it was the first part of the brain to develop and, interestingly, it is also the first part of the brain to develop in a fetus.

The reptilian brain is responsible for all essential-to-life systems such as ensuring that our hearts beats, we continue to breathe and we digest food, etc. We don't have to use any psychic energy for these functions, they just happen automatically. Other functions thought to be controlled by the reptilian brain are territoriality and keeping you and yours safe.

One of the reptilian brain's major functions is to determine what is or isn't a threat. When something is familiar, our reptilian brain will see it as safe and preferred, but it responds with suspicion to anything that is new or a major change. Unless additional information is provided quickly, our reptilian brain will place the situation in the dangerous category. This safety function is part of the reason why it can be difficult to achieve goals or to respond effectively to conflict. If the territory is unknown or makes us uncomfortable, our reptilian brain goes into protective mode, preferring to escape, rather than dealing with something new.

Of special interest to our conflict discussion is the Reticular Activating System (RAS) which is located in our reptilian brain. It is responsible for filtering stimuli so that we are not overwhelmed. You might not have been aware of the sound of your furnace or air conditioner but now that I have mentioned it, you can hear it. Your RAS does that for you. It discards information that it deems unnecessary to your immediate context. This filtering is fascinating because obvious details may never reach your conscious awareness.

Chabris and Simon demonstrated this phenomenon in their book, *The Invisible Gorilla*.[4] They showed participants a video and instructed them to count the number of times the basketball players with white jerseys passed the ball. While the players were passing the ball, a large gorilla walked through the middle of the playing area and even posed before leaving the scene. Interestingly, well over 50% of the observers did not see the gorilla and, when told about it, insisted that it was not there. They had to be shown the video a second time before they would believe it was present! I wonder just how much we miss while we believe that we have truly seen?

Going into a conversation that involves conflict is going to set off the alarms in our reptilian brain. Due to the RAS, we cannot know for sure that we really do have all the critical information when we respond. We cannot trust our own perceptions because they have been filtered. The reptilian brain is all about self-preservation. The facts which grab our attention are those that support the perception that we, or something of value, are at risk. On the other hand, facts that suggest that we might be wrong, or that the other party is not the enemy, are at risk of being missed.

In Chapter 3, we talked about facts versus stories. Since our facts do not represent **all** the facts, our stories are quite likely to be, at least a little, off the mark! Being open to hearing the other person's facts and story may be essential to achieving a good resolution.

The limbic system

The limbic system is often referred to as our emotional brain. This is where long-term memories are stored; it is the seat of our motivations, and the home to our emotions. Our preferences, habits, heuristics, values, memories and learned behavior are all stored here. The limbic system, like the reptilian brain, is ancient. It works with pictures, sounds and smells and does not have access to symbolic language.

A well-worn example illustrates this clearly, "don't think of a pink elephant." Your limbic system immediately visualized a pink elephant but didn't have the capacity for processing the word "don't." The result is you did exactly what the speaker did not want you to do. When you tell your adolescent, "don't forget to take out the trash," you have created an image of the trash in its usual resting place. What do you think is going to happen? In all likelihood, the trash is going to remain in its usual resting place.

Henry Ford was quoted as saying, "if you think you can do a thing, or you think you can't do a thing, you're right." What you visualize, is what your brain works on creating. If you think a conflict is going to go poorly for you, you are visualizing all the bad outcomes and, whether you realize it or not, you begin acting in ways which will make

43

your picture come true. The self-fulfilling prophecy is nothing more than a vivid picture in your head which you act to create, while consciously unaware.

What you think matters! Your limiting beliefs are creating your reality. In 1954, Roger Bannister ran a four-minute mile. An achievement which was, until then, commonly believed to be impossible. Since then over 1,400 runners, and counting, have done what was once considered impossible. I wonder what would happen if you changed your own limiting beliefs about dealing with conflict? I repeat, what you think matters. When you create a different picture in your head, you create a different outcome.

We are usually not consciously aware of the extent to which the limbic system is influencing our decisions, and this has a considerable effect on how we deal with difficult situations. Anything we experience causes a set of neurons to fire. Hebb's Law states that neurons that fire together, wire together. In this manner, pathways are formed which get stronger the more frequently they are used and eventually our responses to specific stimuli become habitual and automatic. This is the basis of both classical and operant conditioning. Conditioning influences our responses to situations, even when we want to respond differently.

I can tell myself that a cream puff is bad for me and that I don't want it but my experience with cream puffs is that they are delicious. From the time I was 12 years old, cream puffs have been paired with sweet loveliness and when I see a cream puff, I am conditioned to put it in my mouth. That's not to say that I can't overcome this conditioning. However, it takes a conscious effort and sometimes, I just don't have the energy to resist. The same happens in countless other situations in our lives.

When my mother was annoyed with my father, she would move the furniture as a way of creating a fresh environment for herself. The endorphins from the physical effort of moving furniture and the dopamine from exerting control over her environment were guaranteed to make her feel better. For me, however, furniture moving signaled tension in the home. To this day I get stressed if furniture in my home is moved for any reason.

Our experiences with conflict, how we feel and how we respond, have been conditioned in the same way. Again, we can consciously overcome this conditioning but first we must be aware that our thinking and actions are a conditioned response. We also need to have the know-how and energy to overcome the conditioning. In many situations this is a one-two punch that is just too much to beat.

The limbic system is actually a compilation of many smaller systems, but the two most relevant to conflict are the amygdala and the hippocampus. One of the main functions of the amygdala is to bring about an immediate response to danger. The thalamus, another structure in the limbic system, receives a stimulus and sends it on to various parts of the brain for processing. When there is an immediate danger, however, this route eats up critical split seconds. That's where the amygdala comes into play. When the thalamus receives a stimulus associated with danger, this stimulus is available right away to the amygdala which then kicks into immediate action with no input from the rest of the brain. If you are out walking and an angry, growling dog steps into your path your body immediately prepares to either defend yourself from the animal or to run. The response is automatic!

The hippocampus is the other part of the limbic system that we need to highlight. This part of the brain encodes the context of our experience: the where, what and when of events. It is also responsible for short-term memory. Without the hippocampus, no new learning is possible. What is that saying: "Fool me once, shame on you; fool me twice, shame on me."? It's the hippocampus that is responsible for this experiential learning. However, when the hippocampus is overwhelmed, this kind of learning does not take place. So, the old adage quoted above isn't always fair! There are circumstances when you will not be able to see opportunities or strategies that are right in front of your eyes because the hippocampus is not functioning well. This has implications for the concept of "learned helplessness" which was first coined by Martin Seligman. It also effects our ability to respond effectively, or even to turn off, our stress response.

The prefrontal cortex

The prefrontal cortex (PFC) is the third brain and is relatively new in the evolution of our species. Interestingly, it is the last part of our brains to develop and is usually not fully functioning until around the age of 25. This is the part of the brain that is responsible for language, abstract thinking, thought analysis, and regulating behavior. The proverbial "willpower" is sourced in the PFC because it is tasked with considering multiple variables and making conscious choices, particularly when there are competing goals. This is the part of the brain which plans, considers potential outcomes and anticipates future events. You can see why the late development of this part of the brain can cause problems for the young adult!

Something happens, such as another person making a comment or doing something that is not to your advantage. First to react is your limbic, always on guard for any potential threat. Then your PFC builds the case with all the reasons why you should be upset. The PFC analyzes and draws conclusions. Often you have already reacted emotionally to the signals that a threat is in the air and then only later the PFC provides you with the justification for your actions. When this happens, your actions can easily violate your core values or, at least, not make your Mama proud. This sequence happens so quickly that your justifications get mixed up with the facts and it is difficult to separate them. This is the facts vs. stories discussed in the previous chapter.

At other times, the signals from the limbic system are low enough that you don't react right away. When this happens, the PFC kicks into action, analyzing all the incoming data and creating a case for which action would be appropriate. When we are lucky, the PFC does a good job and we act in ways that are productive and move us towards our goals.

Unfortunately, as already discussed, your limbic system is sneaky and continues to influence the thinking part of your brain. While you believe you are being rational and logical in the choices you are making, the limbic system is filtering the information which reaches the PFC and coloring that information which does get to our conscious awareness with our heuristics, habits and preferences.

Remember the brain pathways that were discussed earlier? They become so deep and so strong that it is hard to act outside of them. Think of water running over a flat rock. Initially, the water spreads out but over time, the water creates a groove which eventually becomes so deep that the water will only flow through this groove. Behavior patterns that get repeated frequently enough become like that deep groove. When confronted with a situation similar to those experienced in the past, your behavior will fall into the same old groove without conscious, deliberate effort. It's the path of least resistance. Your PFC will then quickly provide you with a rationale as to why you did so and why it was the right thing to do.

I did say that conscious, deliberate effort can help us to avoid falling into old habitual responses that are not helping us. We can create new, more productive behavior paths. That gives us hope, especially for when we are faced with a tense situation. We are not destined to engage in the same behavior we learned as a child and which is often counterproductive to the result we want. We do have a choice. We can use our PFC to help us consider other options, anticipate consequences, create a plan and execute the plan. Yay!

There is a catch though. All of this requires willpower and, it turns out, willpower is not always as available as we would hope. As Kelly McGonigal explained in her book, *The Willpower Instinct*, willpower is not a virtue, it is a biological function.[5] Stress can and does hijack your ability to control your behavior. If you are like me, you may develop a plan for how you intend to respond to a situation. Then something happens and the plan goes straight out the window. Things may come out of your mouth that you never intended to say, and you wish you could take back almost as fast as you said them. Thank You emotional brain, you won again!

The stress response

We want to believe that, as a species, we have evolved well beyond our ancient ancestors. Our living environment is certainly more comfortable. Technology has made a dramatic difference in our mobility and the way in which we communicate with one another. The differences between our lifestyle and that of our ancestors, even just our grandparents, are impressive. Nevertheless, our brain wiring is still the same as our earliest ancestors. This wiring hasn't kept pace with the social changes and the technological advances that surround us.

Our amygdala, the part of the brain responsible for detecting danger, is constantly scanning for potential threat just as it has always done throughout the history of our species. When it detects stimuli that had been associated with danger in the past, it activates the fight-or-flight response of the sympathetic nervous system. Our bodies are flooded with adrenaline and cortisol. The adrenaline provides the energy for the fight-or-flight response. When the sympathetic system is activated, blood and oxygen are diverted to the parts of the body where they are most needed to either fight or run. The cortisol creates a hyper-vigilance for any further signs of threat. Both adrenaline and cortisol are critical survival factors in the presence of danger.

This is all well and good, but the amygdala does not differentiate between perceived or real danger. The fight-or-flight response is in place to help us escape from the proverbial lions, tigers and bears. I don't see many of them in my daily life, but my amygdala is continuously sounding the alarm anyway. Someone cuts me off on the highway, or my boss hands me still another project on an already full plate or the dishes aren't done when I reminded my son three times, and I am in full fight-or-flight mode. Unfortunately, my go-to is more often fight rather than flight and that can cause all kinds of problems.

Our sophisticated, complicated environment is constantly full of triggers. Some threats are real, and survival demands that the amygdala sound the alarm. If a person steps out of an alley with a knife and tells you to turn over your wallet, that's a real threat. Fortunately, this kind of threat is rare. More often, the amygdala is sounding the alarm because the door closed before you got onto the subway, someone sent a not-so-nice gesture your way in the grocery store or your vacuum quit working when you desperately needed to tidy up before the in-laws arrived. Our physical response to threats is the same, whether they are real or perceived.

Our bodies can handle the occasional surge of adrenaline and cortisol, but prolonged or frequent exposure to these hormones has some serious side-effects. Besides causing physical disorders, these side-effects have major consequences for our ability to respond effectively to a tense situation. As it happens, our modern environment is the perfect prescription for prolonged and frequent triggering of the fight-or-flight response. Just think about your responses while watching a child you care about playing in a baseball or soccer game. Does your heart start to pound? Do you ever feel so tense that you have to pace?

Do you find yourself yelling encouragement to the child or something else to the umpire or referee? You are absolutely not in danger, but your body is responding as though you are.

When the amygdala sounds the alarm and your body responds with the flood of adrenaline and cortisol, additional blood and oxygen are supplied to those parts of your body that will need more energy to run or to turn and fight. Your brain is an energy hog. While your brain makes up less than 2% of your body weight, it uses between 20% – 25% of your body's oxygen and energy supply. When you are in full fight-or-flight mode, there is only enough blood and oxygen left in the brain to manage critical functions like breathing and keeping your heart pumping. You are literally dumbed down when you are stressed. Have you ever been in a situation where, an hour after an argument, you think of something you should have said? There is no point in being annoyed with yourself for not thinking of that brilliant point in the moment. You couldn't! You didn't have the brain power when you needed it most.

Over-exposure to cortisol has another consequence. Earlier, I explained that the hippocampus was responsible for processing new learning. If we want to create new pathways in the brain, the hippocampus is our hero. It has another important function and that is to turn off or turn down the stress response. The problem is that cortisol kills the neurons in the hippocampus. For our ancestors, that was not a problem because the hippocampus is also able to generate new neurons.

When the stress response is triggered only occasionally, the hippocampus is perfectly capable of keeping the supply of neurons at an adequate level. However, the stress response is triggered so often in our current environment that the hippocampus can become overwhelmed. When this happens our ability to learn from experience and to build new and more productive behavioral patterns is hampered. Further, the hippocampus' ability to turn off or turn down the stress response when the threat has passed becomes weakened. Once again, when faced with a conflict or even just a tense situation, our ability to benefit from our PFC and all its advanced abstract thinking is seriously compromised.

There is, however, some good news! There is a protein in the hippocampus, Brain Derived Neurotrophic Factor (BDNF) which protects neurons naturally. As John Medina explained in his book, *Brain Rules*, under normal conditions it maintains the functions of the hippocampus, but it gets depleted when constantly exposed to cortisol.[6] Two known behaviors help the body to increase production of BDNF: exercise and mindfulness. We will come back to this in later chapters because it is the key to our being able to take control of our physiology and break through to the results we want.

DOSE and its role in conflict

Much has been written about the neurotransmitters Dopamine, Oxytocin, Serotonin and Endorphins (DOSE) and their role in our feelings of happiness and well-being. When it comes to discussing conflict, however, they also have a downside.

Dopamine

Dopamine is the neurotransmitter that is associated with pleasure, motivation and learning. When we encounter an unexpected good event, dopamine surges through our body, giving us a feeling of pleasure. Hearing the occasional use of your name by a salesperson, seeing an old friend at the store, or achieving something of value to you, will result in a surge of dopamine. It is often referred to as the "more-ish" chemical because we will repeat any behavior that produces a surge of dopamine. It serves as a motivator because we always want more of what will cause its release – more stuff, more stimulation and more surprises.

How does this affect conflict? When you respond to conflict with a well-worn pattern and you see a short-term improvement in your situation, your brain is going to reward you with a surge of dopamine. This will certainly increase the probability that you will repeat the same behavior pattern under similar circumstances, but it might be to your detriment. If the improvement in your situation is short-term, and the consequences only come later, it is unlikely that you will be motivated to learn new, more productive behavior.

For example, Jason reprimands Andrea for errors on her report. Andrea apologizes and promises to work harder. With this response

Jason feels that he has achieved what he set out to get better performance. Do you remember what happens when we are under stress? Jason's reprimand has certainly gotten Andrea's attention but not quite in the way he would have hoped. Andrea is sincere in her desire to do better and works hard to do so but she is working against her own physical stress response. Under stress she has less of the oxygen which she needs to think clearly, and her hippocampus is compromised in its ability to process information. As a result, Andrea is more likely to make mistakes and her ability to solve problems deteriorates. Jason has congratulated himself on his short-term win and, when Andrea makes future errors, which is now highly probable, or fails to find a good solution to a challenge, he is going to fall back on the same pattern of behavior, the reprimand. A very negative cycle can easily develop for both Jason and Andrea.

Oxytocin

Oxytocin is sometimes referred to as the love hormone because it is released in high concentrations during positive social interactions. Oxytocin is the chemical that surges through a mother at the birth of her baby, creating an instantaneous bond and a fierce desire to protect this new little one. Oxytocin is also released when we engage in altruistic behavior or when others are kind to us. It is responsible for the feeling we get when we set eyes on a loved one. It helps us feel connected to others.

Our survival depends on being part of a group, a member of the tribe. There is safety in numbers and when we engage in pro-social behavior, we are accepted by the group and the group provides us with protection. The downside is that it also creates an us vs. them mentality. Once you are part of a group you will work to remain a part of that group and will engage in behavior that will earn you continued membership. In this way, the group influences your values and your sense of right and wrong. You will also work hard to protect the group's continued existence and defend the group against anything which threatens it. Within organizations, many departmental wars are fought over control of resources and oxytocin is a good part of the issue.

Franklin's response to a high-profile project being assigned to another department is a good example of this. While sitting in a meeting, his ears perked up when Rachel announced that her department would take on the CEO's new project. Five new positions would be attached to this project and Franklin had expected that his department would be asked to take it on. He had already been thinking about those additional staff and how, in addition to the CEO's pet project, he could use the additional staff to accomplish other objectives, as well.

Franklin wasn't about to go down without a fight. He and his department needed the additional staff resource and this high-profile project would be good for not only his career, but also the credibility of his department. As soon as the meeting was over, he went into action. He dedicated the next three days to campaigning for a reassignment of the project and when this didn't succeed, he quietly made it difficult for Rachel to get access to critical reports and information which she needed from his department. In the end the project failed and at the same time the organization missed an important opportunity to reposition itself in a changing market.

Does this sound all too familiar? When we see ourselves as part of an in-group and define others as part of an out-group, we can justify behavior that would otherwise be unacceptable. Within organizations the group's objectives become the priority, often to the detriment of the needs of the whole organization. One to one, when we see someone else as a "not me," we are not motivated for any altruistic behavior. Their survival is of no interest to us because we don't feel any connection. As a result, we could engage in behavior that is harmful to them and ultimately to ourselves. In relationships, if one person loses, no one wins. The loser will always try to even the score when an opportunity presents itself, sometimes not even being aware that they are doing so!

Serotonin

When we have optimal levels of serotonin, we feel calm and focused. Serotonin contributes to a balanced mood, relaxation, improved memory and an overall sense of well-being and safety. Low levels of serotonin can result in social withdrawal, loss of interest in social interactions and depression. These ill-effects are often associated with a tendency to take offense easily which puts the individual on the defensive. Social withdrawal isolates the individual from their tribe.

Furthermore, the perception of being attacked can result in the amygdala being in constant heightened alarm mode with all the negative consequences which this has on thinking and problem solving. With low serotonin, the individual is likely to respond with avoidance. Self-fulfilling prophecy can easily come into play, making the perceived attacks become real.

An interaction between Theo and Cole illustrates this. Theo read Cole's email, "I would like to help but I'm swamped. What part of this can you do without me?" Once again, Cole was passing the buck, at least that's what Theo was thinking. Feeling let down, again, Theo buried himself in his work. The next day, Cole sent an email, "Hey, what's up? Where are things at with the AMIST project?" Theo thought to himself, "It's just like Cole to be critical. He doesn't help and then demands an update. I haven't gotten as much done as I need to but I'm not giving him the satisfaction of knowing that." Later in the day, Cole sent another email, "Hey, I'm stuck. I can't go forward without an update. Where are you with the project?" Once again, Theo chose to ignore the request. After all, Cole didn't help him when he had asked him to do so, why should he cooperate with Cole now? The next day Cole showed up at Theo's desk, obviously angry, and in a very abrupt tone demanding an update from Theo. Theo's original fear that Cole was being aggressive and was anything but an ally was now fully realized!

Endorphins

Endorphins, a natural painkiller, is our last stop on this short tour of neurotransmitters. They help us to stay the course when things get tough. This applies as much to emotional as to physical challenges because endorphins moderate the ill-effects of stress and reduce anxiety. When stress and anxiety, are turned down, our expectation for a positive result can increase, thus motivating continued focus and effort. We will feel some level of euphoria when endorphins are flowing, and it is this natural production of joy that has been dubbed "the runner's high."

There are many things that will trigger the release of endorphins, the most famous of which is exercise. Laughter, meditation, visualization, and even dark chocolate or hot, spicy peppers are also good ways to increase your access to endorphins. You need adequate levels of endorphins in your system because depression, anxiety, moodiness and impulsive behavior can easily take hold when levels fall. None of these states are going to be helpful in the presence of conflict or stress as illustrated by Gina's story.

Gina jumped at the chance to take on a high-profile project even though she knew the timeline was tight and she didn't have previous experience with anything this big. After a week of struggling, getting little to no sleep and basically shutting down her whole life to dedicate every possible moment to the project, she hit a problem which increasingly felt unsolvable. With the deadline looming, her supervisor, Hannah, checked in on Gina's progress. Immediately, Gina thought, "She doesn't believe that I can do this and she's probably right. I should just tell her I can't do it!" Fortunately, Gina didn't voice her thoughts. Instead, keeping her doubts to herself, she hurried Hannah off the phone by expressing confidence about meeting the deadline.

Apparently, Hannah wasn't buying it because an hour later she stopped by to ask if Gina was all right. Hannah felt that Gina had been unusually abrupt, and she wanted to offer her help. "I'm fine and I have things under control." Gina told Hannah. Gina regretted not accepting Hannah's help as soon as she left the office. Redoubling her efforts, Gina wondered if it wouldn't be more fair to everyone if she just threw in the towel and gave up. She made up her mind that she would admit her failure first thing the next morning and packed up her things to go home. No need to stay late tonight, she was going to quit anyway.

Once home, Gina went for a run, a luxury she hadn't allowed herself since the beginning of the project. After exercising, Gina felt a little more hopeful and realized that a good night's sleep could only help. The next day she woke up feeling energized and ready to tackle the project again. She wasn't going to admit defeat. In fact, she was going to test out the new idea that had come to her when she woke up. Maybe, just maybe, she could pull this project off after all!

Overcoming our physical response to conflict

Both nature and nurture seem to be conspiring against us when it comes to responding effectively to conflict. But people can and do successfully work through conflict at any of the levels on the continuum from a simple disagreement all the way up to discord. They can get a good result and build their relationships at the same time. How? We already know that the traditional models for conflict management are good, but that they aren't enough.

Over and over, I see people not using the skills which they have in their repertoire. We are not doomed to be victims of our physiology. We can do better. The rider, our logical, rational prefrontal cortex, and the elephant, our emotional brain, need to work together but most often, they don't. Furthermore, we need the tools to help the other party's rider and elephant work together.

Actually, they are working together in some form. The rider thinks he is in control and making the decisions but, as we have discussed, those decisions are heavily influenced by the elephant. To the extent that the rider is cooperating with the elephant, they are working together. That's not what we want. We need the rider to set the direction and the elephant to support that decision. We do not want our elephant or the other party's elephant in control!

The elephant is a powerful source of energy and we need tools to help us direct this energy so that we can achieve important goals. Instead of confronting others, or avoiding them when they resist us, we need tools to employ the elephants in the room effectively. Some would call this being emotionally intelligent, using your emotions to accomplish goals. There is a whole industry that will assess your emotional intelligence but not a lot of solid information about how to improve it. It's time to take back control and the good news is, it's possible! The next four chapters will provide you with specific tools to do exactly that!

Toolkit Summary

- In the absence of clear information otherwise, your mind will go to the dark side and assume that a change in the environment is dangerous.
- Compromising in a conflict is difficult because our wiring motivates us to avoid loss.
- We have three brains, not one: Reptilian, Limbic and Prefrontal Cortex (PFC).
- The primary function of the reptilian brain is self-preservation. It acts instinctively to protect the body.
- The Reticular Activating System (RAS), part of the reptilian brain, filters non-essential stimuli. We are unaware of what is being filtered and this limits our full perception of events.
- The limbic system is the emotional brain. It is the storehouse of memories, habits, heuristics and the source of preferences and feelings. It uses images to process information, not words.
- The limbic system and the reptilian brain combine to form the subconscious brain – the elephant.
- The conscious, logical, rational brain is located in the prefrontal cortex (PFC). This is the rider which is heavily influenced by the elephant. It is usually unaware of the extent of this influence.
- Neurotransmitters heavily influence our feelings and as a result, our thinking. Understanding the effect of Dopamine, Oxytocin, Serotonin and Endorphins (DOSE) and how to increase their production can help us in dealing with difficult conversations.
- One step toward effective conflict management is learning how to get our rider and our elephant working together toward achieving the needed outcomes.

5

Mindset and The Power of "I Am..."

The subtle power of limiting beliefs

I was a middle child in a family of six. My father was career air force which meant that I grew up in private married quarters (PMQs) on Canadian Air Force bases. These homes were row houses and not very big, particularly when you squeezed a large family like ours into one. In a small and crowded home, privacy is not feasible and, even when you didn't mean to, you couldn't help but overhear conversations.

When I was in seventh grade, my father was stationed on an air base in the suburbs of Toronto and I shared a small bedroom with my younger sister, Dana. We got along well and spent a lot of time together at the local library and the strip-mall near the base. Despite our good relationship, I still craved alone time and in our small home, that was hard to come by. Fortunately, I had learned at a very young age that if I had a book, I would be allowed to sit quietly by myself in the living room, where the good furniture was. For me, this was heaven and probably contributed considerably to my love of books.

57

One hot summer afternoon, I was sitting and reading in my favorite chair in the living room, pretty much unnoticed. My mom and her sister were drinking tea in the next room and my ears naturally perked up when I heard my name mentioned in their conversation. I heard my mother say to her sister, "You know, Paula works really hard at her studies, but her grades really don't show that effort. It's not like Dana, she doesn't seem to have to work at all and she is still an A student."

I'm pretty sure my mother did not say I wasn't a good student, but that's what my 12-year-old mind heard. At the time I was a solid B+ student but by the end of the school year, my grades had slipped to a C average. Interestingly, after hearing my mother's comments, I worked harder at my grades, not less! I talked with my teacher about getting extra help and Elaine, my best friend, even tried to help me. Nothing worked. I hoped things would be different at the start of eighth grade but a few weeks into the new year it was apparent that the same pattern was holding. My grades were not looking good.

One thing which was different was that my older brother, David, had started college. Since he was living at home, I would see his textbooks lying around. Being the bookworm that I was, and still am, I couldn't help myself, I had to read them. I became fascinated with his psychology and sociology textbooks and began checking related books out of the public library to learn more about these subjects. My brother noticed the books I was reading and quizzed me to see if I really understood what I was reading. I had apparently passed his test because he said, "I don't get it. You can read this college-level material and understand it better than some of my classmates and yet you aren't an A+ student. You are so smart, but your grades aren't matching. What's going on?"

I didn't have an answer to that question then, but I do now. After hearing what my brother had to say, without making a conscious effort to change anything, my grades began to improve. In Canada, where I went to school, high school was five years, and not four as it is in the U.S. My grades improved so much that I completed the five-year high school curriculum in three years with the equivalent of a 4.0 grade point average. I am not sharing this to impress you; there is an important point to this story. What you tell yourself matters, especially what you tell yourself about yourself.

My brother accidentally freed me from the limiting belief that I was a poor student. When I started to see myself as a good student, things fell into line and that made all the difference. I wonder what limiting beliefs you hold about yourself. When you think about conflict, what are the limiting beliefs that might be interfering with your ability to get the results you need? Are your limiting beliefs encouraging you to settle for more of what you already have and don't want? Are you compromising relationships by either avoiding conflict or by handling it too aggressively because you believe that is your only option?

The impact of negative thinking

Your emotional brain, also known as your subconscious, is listening when you talk to yourself and creating pictures which it then acts on. Telling myself that I was not a good student and working so hard at proving it wasn't true just meant that I had a picture of papers with a big fat C or D on the top or a picture of my parents frowning and looking sadly at my report card. The more I tried to improve, the more I visualized these pictures and the more my subconscious worked towards creating the reality.

That's the thing about your subconscious. Whatever picture you are holding in your head becomes the goal to be achieved. When I don't want something, I have to think about what I don't want and that's the picture I hold in my head. When I replaced what I didn't want with an accurate picture of the books I had been reading and my ability to explain what I was reading, I literally began seeing myself as smart. With the new picture of being smart, I had a different outcome.

There is an old story of two salesmen who were sent to Africa by a British shoe manufacturer to investigate and report back on market potential.

The first salesman reported back, "There is no potential here – nobody wears shoes."

The second salesman reported back, "There is massive potential here - nobody wears shoes."

We can both look at exactly the same thing but, because our filters change what we see, each of us will see it differently. When we think positively, we see opportunities. When our filters are negative, we miss those very same possibilities. It's the same when we think about conflict. If our past experience tells us that we aren't good at handling a particular level of discomfort, we approach it with this negativity and we see it as a problem or a barrier between us and what we are striving for. On the other hand, if we approach the situation with an expectation of success, the same circumstance becomes an opportunity, a challenge we embrace with enthusiasm.

We need to change our thinking if we want better outcomes. The story of McGinty illustrates the devastating effect of allowing negative thinking to go unchecked.

McGinty, a farmer, needed to plough his field before the dry spell set in, but his own plough had broken.

"I know, I'll ask my neighbor, farmer Murphy, to borrow his plough. He's a good man; I'm sure he'll have done his ploughing by now and he'll be glad to lend me his machine."

So McGinty began to walk the three or four fields to Murphy's farm. After a field of walking, McGinty says to himself,

"I hope that Murphy has finished all his own ploughing, or he'll not be able to lend me his

machine..."

Then after a few more minutes of walking and worrying, McGinty says to himself,

"And what if Murphy's plough is old and on its' last legs - he'll never be wanting to lend it to me will he?"

And after another field, McGinty says,

"Murphy was never a very helpful fellow, I reckon maybe he won't be too keen to lend me his plough even if it's in perfect working order and he's finished all his own ploughing weeks ago...."

As he arrives at Murphy's farm, McGinty is thinking,

"That old Murphy can be a mean old fellow. I reckon even if he's got all his ploughing done, and his own machine is sitting there doing nothing, he'll not lend it to me just so watch me go to ruin..."

McGinty walks up Murphy's front path, knocks on the door, and Murphy answers.

"Well good morning Mr. McGinty, what can I do for you?" says Murphy.

And McGinty says, with eyes bulging, "You can take your bloody plough, and you can stick it up your bloody a____!"

Obviously, this is a caricature of the process but, if you are like me, you have probably engaged in similar thinking, even if it was less extreme. The more we think about a difficult situation, the more we can become convinced that it is going to turn out badly for us! Worse, this kind of mental imagery makes the probability of a bad result even stronger.

Self-affirmations as the antidote

The antidote to negative thinking and the easiest way to accomplish this is with a self-affirmation. Stuart Smiley, a character on Saturday Night Live (SNL) in the early 90's, was famous for his simple affirmation: "I'm good enough, I'm smart enough, and doggone it, people like me." SNL was making fun of self-affirmations but now we have the tools to see what is happening in the brain when we engage in repetitive, positive statements. It turns out that they really do slow down our brain waves and help us to relax. With a calm mind comes better quality thinking and just like magic, you are smarter, better, and doggone it, you engage in behavior that people find more likable!

We have an almost constant stream of dialogue running through our heads and much of it is "I am…" type statements. Some of it might be positive, such as "I am happy…," "I'm good at…," "I'm strong and healthy," or "I'm a kind person". For most of us, however, the lion's share of this conversation is negative, for example "I am tired…," "I'm not good at conflict," "I'm going to make things worse," or "I'm going to feel bad when…" Neurons that fire together, wire together. This kind of negative thinking creates pathways to disaster.

When you anticipate a difficult conversation or you find yourself blindsided by one, your mind starts playing your negative programs: "I'm not good at this," "I'm going to lose," "I'm going to feel bad when this is done," "I'm not going to be able to think clearly," or "I'm going to make things worse." You have been practicing these thoughts throughout your life so, of course, they are front and center in times of stress. You will have your own script, but it probably sounds similar to those I just described. The exact words you use don't matter; they all have the same result. The amygdala is on high alert, fight-or-flight is ignited, your heart starts beating faster, your breathing gets shallower, you start sweating and your thinking power starts to deteriorate. Everything you worried would happen, does!

A very important step towards achieving better results in a difficult conversation at any level of the conflict continuum is to retrain your brain. Create a new statement and practice it, over and over, again. The new statement has to be realistic or your subconscious will reject it. Most folks can honestly say, "I am a good person," "I am earnest in my intentions" or "I intend to do the right thing for all involved." If you want to, just adopt Stuart Smiley's statement, "I'm good enough, I'm smart enough, and doggone it, people like me." It doesn't matter what you choose provided that it is a positive statement, and, in your moments of calm, you believe it.

If you want a different result, you will have to do something different. Isn't that the age-old adage? You need to build a new pathway and the time to start is now, before you need it. Repetition, repetition, repetition. Create a new, more positive statement. Joel Osteen's principle is simple: Whatever follows the "I am" will eventually find you. It's not mysterious, it's just science. Create a new, more productive pathway and then, when you need it, you will have access to this new program. A difficult conversation can now trigger a more productive behavioral sequence instead of setting off the amygdala and all that this entails.

Athletes know that given the same physical abilities, the winner will be the one who is mentally tough and who can stay focused and calm under stress. The same applies to conflict. Your mindset when you enter the conversation is critical to your outcome. Later we will add some other behaviors that you can use just before you face a conflict that will make your self-affirmation stronger. For now, just practicing the positive "I am's…" will get you started in re-programming your brain for a better result.

The conscious and subconscious mind

We have talked a lot about the prefrontal cortex which is the logical, rational mind, the rider; the limbic system teams up with the reptilian brain and acting together form the emotional brain, the elephant. These are all different terms for the same thing and now, it is time to introduce still another way of referring to these parts of the brain: the conscious and the subconscious mind. While these two parts of the mind correspond to the physical parts of the brain, using these terms refers more to their function.

The conscious brain is what we are aware of, the part of the brain that holds the constant stream of conversation we have with ourselves and the analyzing, evaluating part of the brain. It is sometimes referred to as the executive function or the critical faculty.

The subconscious brain corresponds to the limbic system and works through images, not words. As the labels suggest, we are aware of the stream of activity in the conscious mind and the activities of the sub-conscious are beyond our direct access or control. The subconscious mind is constantly listening in to the stream of conversation going on in the conscious mind and acting on those messages. Thoughts are repeated, get accepted by the subconscious and become our marching orders.

This is why, once you have developed your self-affirmation, it is so important that it is repeated, repeated and repeated again. This new message must compete for attention with all those years' worth of negative messages. When your subconscious integrates your new message and begins working towards making it happen, you no longer have to depend on your willpower or discipline to achieve your goals or to hold to your good intentions when you enter a conversation! You will be able to stay calm and focused and access your peak performance. While a practiced positive self-affirmation is just one step towards managing your emotions and getting a better result, it is a very important first step.

Building your positive mindset

The time to begin is now, not when you are in the middle of a difficult situation. Pull out a piece of paper and brainstorm the negative things you say to yourself and if you have less than three you are not taking this exercise seriously or your life is much better than mine and I want to trade. Then beside each item, write a counter to the statement. The following are a few examples.

Negative	Positive alternative
I'm tired	I choose to be energized.
I'm not good at conflict	I'm learning better, more useful strategies and I am becoming good at managing conflict.
I'm tense	I am relaxed because I am using my tools and I can control this feeling.
I'm not as smart as ….	I am smart and I am learning how to access my best thinking skills even while under stress.

Do you get the idea? You translate each negative statement to the opposite, but you also add information that makes the opposite believable. If you just simply say, "I am the greatest" a little voice inside your head is going to argue, "No, you're not, [*insert your choice of name here*] is obviously better than you." If you say instead, "I am working on becoming the greatest by practicing every day," that little voice is quiet.

There are a couple of other things to consider when writing a self-affirmation statement:

- use first person – I;
- use the present tense – for example, "I am," or, "I choose";
- make them positive – what you do want, not what you don't want.

Once you have created your self-affirmation, or self-affirmations, you can have more than one, it's time to start using them. Remember, you need repetition to compete with the negative pathways you have built up over time. Repetition is the key if you want a change in behavior to become automatic. Display your new affirmation in places where you will see it often. You might consider using a dry erase marker and writing it on your bathroom mirror. You can place it on the screensaver of your computer and your smart phone. Write it on the back of old business cards and put it on your desk or on your refrigerator door.

Every time you see the affirmation, repeat it to yourself at least once or, even better, do it a few times. You don't want to have to depend on willpower to create a change in your behavior. Willpower resides in the conscious brain and, as we have seen, it is no match for the subconscious. Rebuild your pathways with a positive self-affirmation and you will have automatic habit working for you, instead of against you.

Toolkit Summary

- Our outcomes are often limited by our beliefs. Change your beliefs and you can change your outcomes.

- Negative thinking can become a self-fulfilling prophecy.

- Self-affirmations are an antidote to negative thinking and work to change belief systems.

- The subconscious mind is always listening in on the stream of conversation in the conscious brain.

- The subconscious mind acts on the messages from the conscious brain. What gets repeated, gets accepted.

- Create a self-affirmation statement and practice it. Positive affirmations will build an automatic, positive program that can moderate stress and increase the probability of good outcomes when faced with a difficult conversation.

Plan your Approach

Now that you understand what is happening in your body and your mind when you either anticipate or need to manage a conflict, you can take steps to put yourself in a better place.

So, the next thing to consider is the tools you could use to help you with managing this conflict. The next five chapters will give you a variety of tools to pick from. They include using kindness and language more effectively, applying behavioral science tools, being hypnotic in your interactions, employing the Aiki problem-solving method and finally, engaging the CLEAN/N model for difficult conversations. None of these tools, on their own, will be enough to guarantee success but the more tools you combine, the more you increase the likelihood of a good outcome. Chapter 12 will provide you with a guide for matching tools to the level of conflict you are addressing but, in the end, you will need to choose based on your own comfort level.

6

Kindness Wins!

Changing your dance step

No matter what I proposed during staff meetings, it seemed that Erin would challenge it. We were equals in terms of the organizational hierarchy, but Erin had an advantage. She was a runner and at that time, I was not. At noon, she would run three miles with our manager, and they would talk. I rarely had that one-to-one access and I certainly had not built the same bank of social credit which she had achieved through those daily runs.

The pattern at staff meetings was that I would propose an idea or offer my perspective on something which was being discussed, and Erin would immediately criticize what I had said or propose something else without allowing any opportunity for the group to consider my contribution. I asked Erin, once, why she did this to me and she denied having any idea of what I was talking about. She suggested that I was being over-sensitive and that she was just being a team-player. This wasn't my perspective at all! Weeks went by and things just got worse.

An opening came up for an assistant supervisor and you guessed it, the position was not posted for competition and Erin was simply promoted. Now I was in an even worse position because Erin had some authority over me. My options were limited, with the most obvious being to leave the organization. Instead of resigning, I made up my mind to kill Erin with kindness.

I looked for opportunities to be helpful. I complimented her on her positive outcomes, both privately and publicly when an appropriate opportunity presented itself. Instead of defending my ideas when she contradicted me in a meeting, I looked for the merit in her suggestion. I would then follow with a "yes, if" or "yes, and" tool, which is described in the next chapter, to create further discussion. The "yes, if" technique simply says "yes" to the idea provided certain conditions were true but, since these conditions are not present, how can we adjust the suggestion to make it work? The "yes, and" technique agrees with the idea and adds on to it.

It's very hard to continue attacking or competing with someone who is being genuinely helpful and openly non-competitive. Although it took a few weeks, Erin's attitude towards me improved dramatically. Ten years and two different organizations later, we are good friends. Erin will often touch base with me to get my perspective on something she is working on or just to have a friendly chat.

Whether or not Erin would admit it to me or even to herself, her pattern of behavior was aggressive and competitive. I clearly represented a threat to her and, when this is the case, going head-to-head by confronting or challenging her would only deepen her sense of threat. Given that she had our supervisor's ear, confronting her wasn't going to be a successful strategy, even if I did manage to win a verbal battle. I opted for a completely different strategy instead.

Zig Ziglar argues that the way to get what you want is helping another to get what they want. It occurred to me that if I wanted respect and collaboration from Erin, I needed to give her respect and be clearly collaborative. I also needed to reassess my behaviors to identify what I was doing to create that sense of threat in Erin. When I changed my dance step, Erin changed hers!

The effect of kindness in conflict

There are two critical mechanisms at work when you use kindness to resolve a difficult situation, namely oxytocin and the principle of reciprocity.

When you are kind to someone both you and the recipient experience a surge of oxytocin. As was discussed earlier, oxytocin is often referred to as the "love hormone" because it creates a bond between individuals. Both parties feel more connected to each other when oxytocin is present. They are no longer talking to each other across a wall because they are now both on the same side of the wall.

Oxytocin is a critical factor in forming communities and in pro-social behavior. We are wired to protect members of our personal tribe and, when we do something kind for someone, we are momentarily given entrance to that person's tribe. It might not last long but, while it is present, we tend to be more cooperative with one another. This is why the salesperson in a car dealership offers to get you a cup of coffee or a bottle of water. It's hard, although not impossible, to be mean to someone when you feel some connection with them.

There is another reason why the salesperson offers you a beverage, it's the Principle of Reciprocity. Robert Cialdini describes this in detail in his book, *Influence: The Psychology of Persuasion.*[7] This principle states that we are socialized to expect that people will give back what they have been given, in equal or larger terms. If my sister-in-law sends me a birthday card, I feel some pressure to remember to send her a card on her birthday. The principle of reciprocity does not guarantee that kindness will be returned with kindness, but the probability is high.

When the salesperson gets you a beverage you are going to be more inclined to accept his offer or at least not be as aggressive in your negotiations. Likewise, when I listened to Erin's ideas in a meeting, she became more inclined to return the favor and listen to mine. Once I set up a pattern of kindness, she frequently behaved in a kind manner in return. Over time this brought the principle of consistency into the mix, but we will discuss consistency in a later chapter.

Being soft vs. being kind

When I suggest to people that they should use kindness as a way of resolving an ongoing conflict, I usually get responses like: "Won't people take advantage of me?"; "People will think I'm soft."; "Doesn't the other party have some responsibility, shouldn't they have to be kind, too?"; "Isn't that being manipulative?" Let me be clear. I am not suggesting that kindness is the answer to all conflicts, nor even most. I live in this world, too! But it is a tool in your toolbox and a really good tool for the right situations; if nothing else, it feels good when you are using it because it gets your oxytocin flowing.

Let's address the objections I get to using kindness as a tool, beginning with the last one. Being manipulative means that we are managing or influencing behavior in *an unfair manner*. You are being manipulative when you are adapting or changing something to suit your own purpose or to gain an *advantage*. When I was being deliberately kind to Erin, I did so with the hopes that it would change her behavior towards me and that she would be more kind in return. So, while my kindness would obviously be to my advantage in the long run, my acts of kindness were focused on helping Erin achieve her goals and feeling good about herself. It fostered growth and confidence. I'm not sure how you could argue that I was being unfair or changing my behavior strictly to my advantage because the benefit to her was immense.

Eastern philosophy has long talked of the concept of karma, that whatever you do comes back to you, whether good or bad. This is another way of describing the principle of reciprocity. Nevertheless, you shouldn't ever do things for others strictly to get something in return. People feel this and they resent it. It just doesn't work. If, however, you are kind towards someone with a sincere heart and because you care, karma comes into force. You are building social credit. When you need help, those people with whom you have built this bank of social credit will want to help you. They will choose to return your kindness. Not because they owe you, but because they now care about you and want to be helpful. What's the old saying, "You scratch my back and I'll scratch yours."

Worry about being taken advantage of or being concerned that people might think you are soft is sourced deep within your subconscious. It comes from a fear that you are on your own, that you are not fully accepted by your tribe and that they will not step up and protect you when you need it. The fear of being isolated from the tribe is deep. In ancient cultures, the worst punishment inflicted on a person was for the whole community to treat them as though they were dead. They wouldn't talk to the person and would look right through them as if they weren't there. Inevitably, the person died within a few days, despite the fact that food, water, and shelter were still available. We desperately crave a sense of belonging and, in those cultures, being treated as a non-being was a death sentence.

It is ironic that the very behavior needed to reduce the fear that the tribe will not be there for you is the behavior which you are resisting. When you reach out and help someone else, your body is rewarding you with oxytocin, helping you to feel more connected to the other person. At the same time their body is responding with the same hormone and they are feeling, at least momentarily, more connected to you.

Using kindness in a conflict situation isn't a perfect system. It may take several acts of kindness to break through the suspicion or mistrust that has become part of your relationship with the other person. However, if you stay the course, you will see results. If you don't see the change in behavior after giving it your best effort, then feel free to try something else.

What about the other party's responsibility? Their behavior is hurtful or just wrong. Why should I go first? The answer to that question is easy. Someone must go first if you are going to change the dance step. Since you can't change anyone's behavior but your own, you might as well get it started. Make the first move towards a different relationship and watch the other party change their step. If they don't, you still have the option of doing something else but what if resolving the conflict were as easy as just being kind? How cool would that be? Your self-image as a good person improves and your work gets easier because you are collaborating instead of fighting or avoiding.

The authors of *Crucial Conversations* argue that people resist you not because they don't care about you but because they believe you don't care about them or about the things they care about. When you take off the gloves and focus on showing that you do care, many problems dissipate.

Being deliberately kind feels good, makes the world a little better, and often reduces or eliminates an ongoing conflict. It's worth a try!

Being honest

Some folks think that to be kind they can't be honest. They believe that to be kind they need to soften or hide their truth because they don't want to hurt the other party's feelings. Not being honest is not being kind. The other party needs to understand what you are feeling or thinking for them to be able to adjust their behavior. If you don't share this information with them, they will continue with their behavior and your tension will build. Then one day, your truth explodes and you say or do things which are usually well out of proportion to the context, are counter-productive to a good result, and damaging, at least temporarily, to the relationship. This is not what you want.

By the same token being honest and sharing your truth is not a license to be cruel. Compassion and truth are firmly tied. Without compassion, truth is hurtful. While it serves the speaker, it harms the listener. However, compassion without truth is just being nice. Nice is not the same as kind. Being nice is focused on being pleasing and agreeable. Being kind might include being pleasing and agreeable, but it isn't always. Being kind means the underlying motivation for the action is to be helpful, giving, and/or caring. While honesty and truth are essential components of managing conflict, they must be presented in a compassionate manner.

Forgiveness

The ultimate kindness is forgiveness. When you have been hurt by someone it's hard to think of forgiveness because the word is misunderstood. The phrase "forgive and forget" is a major culprit in this misunderstanding because it suggests that you should let the transgression go, as if it never happened.

First, the brain doesn't work like that. It is always on guard for a potential threat and, when it does happen, it files the incident away so that it can sound the alarm if anything similar occurs. Second, if we are able to forget the incident, and we are most likely just blocking the memory and not really forgetting it, we lose any opportunity to learn and grow from the incident. What a waste! Finally, the phrase "forgive and forget" implies that the relationship will return to previous levels of trust and caring. This concept of reconciliation could be a part of forgiveness, but it is not necessary and should not be expected. We do not have to accept more of the same harmful behaviors which this party has dealt us; this is exactly what we set ourselves up for when we insist on reconciliation.

According to the dictionary, forgiveness simply means that we cease to feel resentment against an offender. That's all! We let go of the pain. We don't allow the hurt to continue. You don't forget or even excuse the behavior. You just lessen the grip of the hurt and free yourself from being controlled by the other party who had harmed you. This is easier said than done but forgiveness is not for the other person; forgiveness is a gift to yourself. If you don't forgive, you continue to dwell on the hurt and you hurt again, and again. The hurt becomes resentment, anger, bitterness and a sense of injustice. You deepen your victimization and it can swallow you up. The hurt robs you of your joy and happiness as its negativity crowds out your awareness of the positives which are available in the present moment. Why would you give your transgressor so much power over you? You deserve better and you can have better!

Robert Enright, in his book, *Forgiveness is a Choice,*[8] offers a four-step process for forgiving.

1. **Uncover your anger.** Instead of blocking or denying your anger, turn and face it. Allow yourself to feel it and seek to understand why you are feeling angry. What is it about the incident that is causing your hurt, what is the loss or the threat?

2. **Make the conscious decision to forgive.** You can do this by consciously recognizing how your feelings are harming you and that just ignoring or coping with them is not working for you.

3. **Develop compassion for the offender.** That doesn't mean that you excuse the behavior, but you do recognize that they

73

are just trying to get by in the same way that you are. Unfortunately, the path which they took caused harm and that is not acceptable. You lessen the sense of "not me" when you realize that they are a human being dealing with their own history of hurt, pain, and fear. Once you feel some sense of connection, even at a very, very basic level, it helps you to let go of the hurt.

4. **Release the harmful emotions by reflecting on how you have grown from the experience.** Yes, you are looking for the "silver lining" and sometimes it is very hard to see in the short-term. You might want to picture yourself ten years from now, looking back. What does this older version of yourself see? The person you are now is the sum of all of your experiences, the good and the bad.

Enright's steps are solid, and you will help yourself immensely if you are able to put them into practice. Notice that I said, "if." This model has one drawback. It is taking a cognitive, logical, rational approach to a situation that is emotional and as a result, illogical and irrational. Some people can execute the four steps successfully but for most, more is needed. Calming the elephant before attempting these steps will allow you to take a whole brain approach to achieving true forgiveness. To do that I offer you a self-hypnosis recording to help you ease into full forgiveness.

To download the recording, go to
https://conflictatworkbook.com/resources/.

Toolkit Summary

- You can be kind and still protect your interests.
- Be the first to change the dance – help others get what they want.
- Kindness improves relationships by creating a sense of connection between parties.
- The principle of reciprocity comes into effect with kindness. When you are kind, others feel some pressure to return kindness to you.
- Being kind is not being soft. You can be kind and still protect your interests and be firm with others.
- Being kind does mean being honest. You can be honest without being mean.
- Forgiveness is a kindness you show yourself.

7

Decoding and Using Language Effectively

Speaking in code

When I first moved to the U.S. from Canada, I thought I spoke the same language. I now proudly proclaim that I am bilingual, I speak both Canadian and American. We take it for granted that when we use a word, the other person is creating the same picture in their head as we have in ours.

My youngest son was in kindergarten when our family moved to Kansas. Not long after, his new teacher was insisting that we have him tested for a developmental disability because it seemed that he was unable to follow simple instructions. "It's not like we speak different languages!" she exclaimed. I asked her for an example of a simple instruction which he was unable to follow and she said, "I asked him to put the sack in the trash and when he looked confused, I asked him to hand me the sack, to which he began examining his hand." I had to explain that in Canadian you would have needed to tell him to put the bag in the garbage and, oh by the way, telling someone to "hand me" something is a colloquialism that he would not have heard in the suburb of Toronto, where he was raised.

When we speak to others, we believe that we are communicating clearly. The other person might even nod their head to indicate that they understood what you have said. This is the big issue in communication; we think that we are speaking the same language, but we are actually speaking in code. Take, for example, the simple phrase, "He beat me." This statement could mean that he won a competition against me, that he hit me repeatedly, or that he got somewhere faster than me. Perhaps there are even more meanings, but you get the point.

We rely on the context to help us interpret the meaning of what is said, but sometimes the context is just not enough. A few years back I commented to a colleague, "We ought to celebrate this accomplishment." Much to my surprise, a couple of days later, I discovered that this colleague was planning a party to "celebrate." I simply meant that we should pause, call attention to the achievement, and consciously congratulate ourselves. There was a big difference between what I meant and what my colleague understood.

We speak in code and we don't realize that we are doing so. We are often speaking in code when we use adjectives or adverbs and this can have serious consequences where misunderstandings could graduate on the conflict continuum to full-blown discord.

Breaking the code

The challenge, especially when tension is already in the air, is to remember that we all speak in code. We use a language that is specific to our experiences and we need to remember that others will decode our communication based on their own personal language.

Active listening is a good start. None of us do enough of that. If you are like me, unless I deliberately catch myself, I will be listening for my next opportunity to respond and not really listening to what the other person is saying. Or, I will be formulating my rebuttal while not really listening to understand. When we listen actively, not defending or interrupting, it's like getting the exam questions ahead the actual exam. This additional information can be added to what you already have and, quite likely, change your perspective, before you begin speaking.

When someone is upset and you respond with active listening, they will usually run out of negative energy after three to five minutes. Don't trust me on that, test it out yourself! The next time someone is upset, wait before you add anything to the conversation. Active listening doesn't mean you don't say anything. It does mean that you don't begin "fixing" the issue or defending your position before hearing what the other person has to say. You encourage the other party to keep talking by using filler words and nods, you ask questions for deeper understanding, and you paraphrase what you heard to confirm that you heard correctly.

Asking questions for deeper understanding is great advice but it is often done poorly. Use the wrong tone of voice and it sounds like you are challenging what the other party had just said or, worse, that you are making fun of them. Use a closed question and you get a one- or a two-word answer that doesn't bring you any closer to understanding what the other party is trying to communicate. The key to breaking the code of another person's communication is to recognize what might be a code word and asking an open-ended question. For example, "When you said that you expected the report to be done, what does 'done' look like from your perspective?" You cannot assume you know what a person means when they say they are frustrated, tired, anxious, hurt, or even happy! Any adjective or adverb can potentially lead you astray, particularly if there is any level of tension present.

Wendy Sullivan and Judy Rees, in their book *Clean Language,*[9] suggest using what they refer to as "ultra-open-ended" questions. These are questions that are free from any assumptions and metaphors and allow the speaker maximum freedom to choose how they answer. Questions like, "…and then what happens?"; "…what would you like to have happen?" or "When you say you are frustrated, what is 'frustrated' for you?" My personal favorite is, "What else can you tell me about [whatever it is we are talking about]…?" When you are in a situation in which a misunderstanding has the potential for conflict, or you recognize that the conversation has already spiraled down into conflict, decoding another person's communication is essential. This requires:

- listening attentively;
- remembering that you are probably speaking a slightly different language and that you need to check your understanding of the adjectives, adverbs, and metaphors which the other party is using;

- asking open-ended questions; and, finally,
- asking more questions based on the answers you get.

Making these four steps part of your natural response to tension with another party will take practice but it's worth the effort. From my experience in coaching managers, so many disputes could have been avoided or minimized if they had checked their understanding of the other party's communication or had clarified their own.

Language patterns

Language is a big deal and we often underestimate the impact of our choice of words and phrases. While you were growing up, certain words word or phrases were used frequently within specific contexts. This frequent pairing conditioned you to respond to these words and phrases with a predictable reaction. Some evoke a positive response; others, a negative one. I call these magic words and phrases because they are producing a consistent response although you are usually not consciously aware of the impact which they are having on your emotions.

Words and phrases that create a positive, energizing effect I refer to as **sparks**. Those words that have the opposite effect of either provoking you to shut down and withdraw mentally from the conversation or which create anger, frustration, or a sense of victimization, I refer to as **triggers**. Everyone has their own mix of sparks and triggers, depending on their experience. There are, however, many sparks and triggers that are common to most people raised in a Western culture and it is worth identifying them.

Trigger words and phrases are a problem in tense situations because, without realizing it, we are more likely to use them during these discussions. When we do, we increase the sense of threat in the other person and thus make the situation even more difficult. We tend to use these words and phrases when we feel some level of threat because they make us feel like we have more control. Unfortunately, they have the opposite effect because they provoke the other party to increase their own resistance to us.

Some examples of the most common triggers and sparks and how they work are described below, but these lists certainly do not include all

79

possible examples. Depending on your experience, some words would have a bigger impact than others on you personally. There are some triggers and sparks that are truly unique to you and are not listed here. After reviewing this list of common triggers and sparks, it might be useful to take some time to think about which words or phrases serve as a trigger or spark for you. It would also be useful to watch for when and where you are using the common triggers and sparks and to notice what response you are getting from the other party.

Trigger words and phrases	How and why they provoke increased resistance
Universals such as: always, never, every, all, nobody, everybody, and everything.	When one of these words is used, the other party stops listening to what you are saying and begins scanning their experience for the exception. For example: "You never take out the trash." "That's not true. On December 17th, 2017 I took out the trash." This example is an exaggeration, but it does demonstrate the extremes we will go to, to prove that the speaker is wrong. If we can provide ourselves with evidence that the speaker is not credible, we can feel justified in dismissing their perspective on other issues. A universal word will rarely hold up under scrutiny because they are almost impossible to prove!
Absolutes such as: avoidable, certain, correct, defective, exact, harmless, incomplete, inevitable, irrefutable, literally, necessary, needless,	Words that represent an absolute judgment, something which is or isn't, will usually evoke a push back from the other party. When the judgment leaves no "elbow-room," the other party will defend their position. A judgment is just an opinion,` or a conclusion and the other party is quite likely

obvious, superior, total, temporary, thorough, unavoidable, unequal, unimportant, universal, valid, worst and wrong.	to have a different opinion or conclusion, particularly about the degree of something. For example: "That was a total waste of time." "I think there were parts of that presentation that were useful to me." The most common offenders are included in this list of absolutes and it is by no means complete.
Why?	This is a perfectly appropriate word in most circumstances, but it is almost guaranteed to create defensiveness if you use it when there is tension between you and another party. From the time you were very little, an adult would ask you a "why" question if they were annoyed or upset with you: "Why did you give the dog your vegetables?"; "Why didn't you clean your room?"; "Why is your homework not done?"; "Why are you late for curfew?" This list of examples could be endless. Your parents, teachers, coaches, supervisors, all did the same thing. When your performance was not at the expected level, the authority figure was likely to ask you "Why?" The result of all this experience is that when we hear the word in any context in which there is tension our amygdala goes on high alert. We immediately recognize that there could be trouble and become defensive.
Just and At least	"Just" is a tricky word because, depending on the context, it can mean a lot of different things and usually it isn't a problem as in: "I just got here"; "I'll just be a minute"; "It was just three dollars!" It's when the word is

	used to minimize something that it can cause a problem. For example: "I was just trying to point out...." This sentence suggests that the listener is making something more of what is being said. "Could you just do it?" suggests that whatever it is you are asking, is not a big deal. If you just did it, things would be better! The listener is quite likely to have another opinion when the word "just" is used to minimize their experience. "At least" has the same effect. It is used to lessen the effect of a sentence and, in a tense situation, the listener is not likely to appreciate the inference. "Could you at least give it a chance?" suggests to the other party that that they are not being fair in their resistance. A perfect recipe for further resistance!
Demands: You need to..., You have to..., You should..., and You must....	Phrases that imply a requirement evoke that little voice in the back of our heads that says, "You aren't the boss of me." Having control over our environment is a basic need. It's what drives a little one to pull the spoon from your hand even though the child has not yet developed the coordination to steer that spoon to their mouth. When we are in control, things are more predictable. With increased predictability comes the capacity to foresee where and when a threat might occur, and this allows us to take proactive steps to protect ourselves. We feel vulnerable when someone else is in control and the result is that we resist others telling us what we must do, or should do.

But, however.	Although "but" can be used in many ways, when we are in a tense situation, the word is almost always used to negate whatever preceded it. For example: "I love your attitude, but I really need to see more cooperation." When we hear something like this we discount or disregard the first half of the sentence and focus on the second half. "However" works the same way; it's just the "city cousin" of "but"! In tense situations "but" or "however" always signal that a reprimand, criticism or demand is about to follow
Don't take this personally, Don't be defensive, and Don't take offense at this.	Any phrase preceded by the word "don't" is a warning that something unpleasant, a reprimand or criticism, is about to follow. In a previous chapter I explained that when we are told not to think about something, we must actually think about it to **not** think about it. It's the proverbial, pink elephant. You weren't thinking about it, but if I tell you not to think about a pink elephant, you picture it immediately. Telling someone to not take something personally or not to take offense works the same way. You just warned them that whatever you are about to say **is** probably offensive or personal.

Spark words and phrases	How and why they create less resistance
Your name.	When you see or hear your name in a novel or unexpected context a surge of dopamine immediately follows. During a difficult conversation, you can use this knowledge by saying the other party's name in a soft and

	caring manner. It will work the opposite, however, if you don't get the tone right.
I wonder, and imagine	These words appeal to the subconscious. They evoke a picture or visualization and, in doing so, bypass the critical, analytical and judging prefrontal cortex that works with words and numbers.
Because.	Our history with the word "because" is that it is usually followed with a logical, rational reason for something. When we hear the word, we tend to get a little lazy and don't always analyze the merit of whatever follows.
Perhaps, maybe, and you might	These words work well when you want to offer advice because they create the illusion in the other party that, when they follow your suggestion it is their decision and that they are in control.
Yes, and.	When you respond to something the other party has said with "yes" the other party recognizes that you are not opposing their idea. This removes the need to be defensive and allows you to add an additional thought to their suggestion. Example: "I think we need to repeat the marketing campaign we used last year." "Yes, and if we add some tweaks to it based on the new data, I think we would have a winner."
Yes, if.	"Yes, if" is a cousin to "Yes, and". The difference is that it adds a condition to the agreement. For example: "I think we need to repeat the marketing campaign we used last year." "Yes, I would agree if we were dealing with the same market issues. Since

	the new data shows some very different trends, we might need to …."
You probably already thought of this…, and You probably already know ….	When you use either of these phrases, you are basically saying to the other party that you believe they were smart enough to already have considered something or to know something. This signals respect and mitigates resistance because if the other party tells you no, they didn't think of X or that they didn't know X they are admitting that they are not smart enough!
Easily, naturally, and automatically.	If something is easy, natural or automatic, there is no reason to resist. We are much more likely to cooperate if we have reason to believe that it will not take a lot of effort and that we can anticipate success.

You can improve your ability to resolve a conflict by using these spark works or phrases. Using trigger words or phrases can exacerbate the conflict. The choice is yours. It will take practice to notice when you are using sparks and triggers but, when you do become aware, observe the other party's response. After a while, it will become second nature to substitute some key sparks for triggers and I promise you, it will make a difference in your difficult conversations.

Body language

It might come as a surprise to you, but your first language was not your mother-tongue. Your first language was body language. As a baby you learned how to influence the behavior of the giants around you with cries and gurgles. Later you added laughing, pointing, and gestures. You also learned to read the giant's body language. You knew when they were upset, happy, or about to put you down for a nap you didn't want! Body language is far more complex than the simple "crossed arms means defensiveness" and guess what? It does, and it doesn't. Sometimes people are just cold or need to do something with their arms!

You are reading and responding to body language all the time, although you might not be consciously aware of it. When people say that they have a "gut" feeling about something, it's usually because their subconscious has noticed and is responding to a subtle body language signal.

Bill Clinton rose to his presidency as a master of body language. Those who met him said that he had a way of making them feel as though he really cared about them. While Mr. Clinton had mastered those elements of body language which are under conscious control, he, like all of us, could not control those elements that are hard-wired and automatic. Experts identified over ten body language indicators or "tells" that he was lying about his relationship with Monica Lewinsky in his testimony to the Independent Counsel. Interestingly, in a survey of non-experts on the day after his testimony there was an overwhelming belief that he was lying. Even when you don't consciously translate body language, your subconscious understands and is responding to it. The general public might not have been able to explain exactly why they thought Mr. Clinton was lying in this testimony but they knew it in their "gut."

There are some good books available if you want to get better at consciously reading other people's body language. For the purpose of conflict management, however, it is important that you understand that body language is a part of any interaction between two people. Moreover, if a person's words do not match the signals which their body is sending, you will always trust their body language over their words. It was your first language and it's your more trusted language.

You don't have to be an expert in body language but being aware of and adjusting for some of the more basic signals will help you during difficult conversations.

There is a difference between the body language signals for dominance compared to those for power. Dominance will immediately put the other party on the defensive when we signal power it bolsters our confidence and creates, subconsciously, a level of respect in the other party. An exaggerated lean forward or stepping into the other party's space is going to signal dominance and this will not help in moving the conversation forward. Likewise, finger pointing or jabbing, even if just in the air, is not going to be helpful. You don't want to engage in either of these and if you observe them in the other party, you will need to deploy some de-escalating gestures, or the safety tools as discussed in chapter 11. If you don't, the conversation is going to spiral out of control very quickly.

An obvious sign that someone is feeling threatened is a raised voice or quickened speech. The threat is unmistakable whenever these behaviors are combined. Engaging in these behaviors during a difficult conversation is usually an attempt to assert control or dominance and, for this reason they are consistently met with resistance in one of two forms: withdrawal or aggression. Neither of these outcomes is going to help in managing the conflict.

A more subtle response is when the voice is lowered and more deliberate and the pace of speech is slowed down. Depending on the way this is done, it can signal either dominance or power. If the lowered volume and slower pace is accompanied by any other sign of resistance, it will be interpreted as a signal of dominance. However, this could also demonstrate that the speaker is in control of their emotions and is carefully deliberating each word. If you lower your voice and speak more slowly, the listener must listen more carefully to hear what is being said and the measured speech can lower the energy of the conversation.

Provided this change in volume and pace is **not** accompanied by any other gestures of dominance, it can signal that the speaker is powerful but is not going to use the power against the listener. This can help to de-escalate the conversation. Don't try this if you don't think you can control your dominance signals because it will make things worse. If, however, you are aware of those body language signals which you can control consciously, and you do so, the lowered and slower speech is a very effective tool.

An easy thing to adjust is body positioning. If you are standing and the other person is sitting, you are signaling dominance. If you are sitting and they are standing, you are signaling vulnerability or weakness. Ideally, you want to be at the same level as the other party. If they are sitting, you should sit down. If they are standing, stand up. Easy! Less obvious is angles. Face-to-face can be intense and could easily set off alarms that threat is in the air. You need to be able to make eye contact, but you want to be in a position to break eye contact comfortably. When possible, place yourself at a 90° angle to the other party. This will allow the needed eye contact without the element of focused eye contact.

Having eye contact is important because it signals to the other party that you are engaged in the conversation. However, extended contact can be aggressive. Ideally, you should maintain eye contact when the other party is speaking, and you break contact briefly when you speak. Making eye contact for very short bursts only, or not at all, will signal that you are weak or that you are hiding something. Neither of these are desirable messages in a difficult conversation.

Posture

Amy Cuddy, in her book, *Presence*,[10] describes the research on power poses. She recommends using a Wonder Woman pose before any stressful event such as a job interview or a presentation. According to Dr. Cuddy, this posture takes up maximum space and delivers a message directly to the brain that you are confident and in control. I would add that it is also a good strategy to use right before a difficult conversation. You can use a less dramatic version by simply sitting with your back touching the back of a chair, your arms resting on the chair arms, your chin slightly up, and your feet flat on the floor. Try it now and see how it feels.

Furthermore, it's important to note that these power poses signal as much information to others as it does to yourself. Taking up more space by sitting with uncrossed arms and legs, shoulders back, and chin up, is a clear signal to others that you are confident and in control. It changes their perception of you. While it is not an aggressive posture, it delivers the message that you are to be respected.

Adjusting your posture to incorporate a power pose is a simple thing that can do no harm. Research suggests that it can have a positive impact on your self-image and others' perceptions of you. An additional bonus is that the good posture which comes with a power pose improves blood circulation in your muscular and skeletal systems. If you know you are going to have a difficult conversation or, perhaps there is a particularly contentious issue that will be discussed in an upcoming meeting, you can slip into a bathroom stall and use a power pose for a few minutes or just adjust your posture in your desk chair for a few minutes prior to the meeting. Furthermore, if you are blindsided by an unpleasant conversation, it would be easy to adjust your posture without calling attention to yourself. You have nothing to lose but, potentially, much to gain!

Stories

Long before we had the written word, stories were the mechanism for handing down knowledge. Storytelling dates back at least 27,000 years to the drawings on cave walls. It is a fundamental communication method which allows us to learn from the experiences of others. Our brains are wired for stories. When we hear a story, the word-processing parts of our brain, the Broca's and Wernicke's areas, are activated. The bonus is that all the other parts of the brain which would normally be set off if we were experiencing the events in the story are also activated. The story creates images in the brain, which engages the emotional brain and it's like we are living the story in real life. This allows us to extract the message of the story and make it our own. Also, while a story is being shared, the brains of the storyteller and the listener become synchronized.

Storytelling is a powerful tool for managing conflict. If you want another person to change their behavior, help them to feel what you are feeling. Stories create empathy and it is through empathy that real change can occur. When you share a story, the listener extracts the message and makes it their own. It literally plants ideas, thoughts and emotions into the listener's brain. Telling a group how many people in their community have died from Covid-19 will not create a lot of behavior change. You will, however, get a different result if you share a true story about a specific person. Without being explicitly told to do so, the listener puts themselves into the story and feels the loss. This is particularly effective if the person in the story is similar, in some way, to the listener. Preparing for a difficult conversation with a story or two can change the outcome dramatically.

Toolkit Summary

- We think we speak the same language as others but we actually speak in code.
- Adjectives and adverbs are usually code words. Our definition of a word will differ from that of others.
- Conflict often results from a misunderstanding of code words.
- Conflict can be avoided or resolved by taking four steps to break the code.
- We are conditioned to respond negatively to some words and phrases – these are called triggers and they shut down thinking or induce resistance or withdrawal.
- We are conditioned to respond positively to certain words and phrases – these are called sparks because they evoke energy.
- Conflict will be managed better if triggers are avoided and more sparks are added to the conversation.
- Body language is our first language and when the message from body language and symbolic language are in conflict, we will trust the message provided by body language.
- Manage your body language to avoid sending threatening messages to the other party.
- Notice the other party's body language and if there are signs that they are feeling fear or a threat, de-escalate the situation.
- Use power poses to increase your self-confidence when you anticipate a conflict or another stressful event.
- Stories create images and this engages the emotional brain. With the emotional brain engaged, changes in behavior are more likely to occur.

8

Behavioral Science and Conflict

Conditioned behavior

Our understanding of why conflict can be so difficult would not be complete without an examination of classical and operant conditioning. Earlier, we had a lengthy look at the how nature influences our behavior through our physiology. But our experiences also influence our behavior and so we also need to examine how nurture affects our responses.

Any discussion of conditioning needs to begin with classical conditioning. Pavlov, in his seminal studies, demonstrated that when an otherwise neutral event is frequently paired with an event that naturally triggers a physical response, the neutral event eventually produces the same physical response as the naturally occurring event.

For example: unexpected, loud noises naturally trigger a startle response. If it happens that you sit at your desk with your back to the door and every time your supervisor enters your office he does so with a loud, booming voice, over time your supervisor will become paired with the startle reflex. With enough pairings you might even startle at the sight of your supervisor and that, in turn, will set off the alarms in your amygdala! This is not good for your relationship with your supervisor or your ability to have meaningful conversations about your work or your personal development. The opposite can also occur. If meetings with your supervisor are often accompanied by music that you find calming, your supervisor could, over time, become associated with feelings of calmness. Now the reverse happens. Just seeing your supervisor could evoke feelings of calm! Classical conditioning can occur at work, but it is the exception, not the rule.

Operant conditioning is related to classical conditioning and is probably more relevant to our discussion of conflict at work. This kind of conditioning can happen accidentally but is more often used deliberately to create a specific outcome. Parents use it all the time, beginning with potty training when a child is heavily praised and rewarded for using the toilet. When parents reward a desired behavior and punish an undesired behavior, they are using operant conditioning to teach their child important lessons.

Operant conditioning is a simple A – B – C sequence. Something happens – the **A**ntecedent. There is a response to what happened – **B**ehavior. The response to the antecedent then produces a result – the **C**onsequence.

For example: you ask your adolescent to mow the lawn – the antecedent. Miracle upon miracle, your adolescent mows the lawn – behavior. You respond by thanking your adolescent or maybe even adding some money into the mix. This would be a reward sequence, assuming that your adolescent likes to be thanked by you or enjoys getting money. Let's follow the same sequence a little differently. You ask your adolescent to mow the lawn – antecedent. Your adolescent is annoyed at being asked and says no – behavior. As the responsible parent you find this behavior unacceptable. You pick up the car keys and announce that they will be returned when the lawn is mowed – consequence. Assuming your adolescent does not like losing access to the car, you have punished the refusing behavior. Operant conditioning is based on the basic law that, given similar conditions, we tend to repeat behaviors which resulted in something pleasant and we avoid behaviors which resulted in unpleasant or painful events. Rewards increase behavior and punishment decreases behavior.

Much of our socialized behavior is created through this simple mechanism. A reward is, by definition, anything that increases the probability of a behavior and a punisher is anything that decreases the probability of a behavior. This is important to understand because something that is socially endorsed may or may not be perceived as a reward.

For example: you complete a difficult assignment and your supervisor makes a big deal about it in front of your teammates. If you are not comfortable with being the center of attention, praise that was intended to be a reward can work as punisher. Another example might be the student who is frustrated with math and distracts himself with disruptive behavior in the class. The teacher sends the student for time out in the hall and now the student has temporarily escaped from that unpleasant math assignment. What was intended as a punishment is quite likely experienced as a reward!

This means that you cannot simply categorize certain behaviors as rewards and other behaviors as punishers. It is not difficult to see this dynamic happening at work, as well. For example, a supervisor assigns a challenging project to a reluctant direct report. The direct report puts little effort into the project and the supervisor reassigns the project to a go-to team member. The reluctant direct report is rewarded for lackluster effort by being relieved of an unpleasant task and the high performing employee may feel punished for past good work by being assigned more and more projects.

Conditioning in action

Anna's story provides another easy example of operant conditioning in action. Anna responds to questions or challenges to her ideas with sarcasm or ridicule. It doesn't take long before people avoid questioning or challenging her. She might not have many friends at work but, on the upside, she gets her own way on projects. Her colleagues are punished for questioning her or attempting to have a deep discussion about issues and Anna is rewarded by their reluctance to engage her in discussions. This is a dangerous dynamic. Anna is engaging in "willful ignorance" by creating conditions under which decisions are being made without the benefit of all relevant information being shared!

Dr. M. Paula Daoust

We are responding to stimuli in our environment all the time. When anything happens, our emotional brain is quickly scanning for previous patterns and immediately assigns an evaluation of good/bad, safe/dangerous, or like/don't like. Your history with rewards or punishment heavily influences this evaluation and you are usually unaware of it.

This can happen in a simple situation like being introduced to someone and feeling immediately on edge. Why? Perhaps this person resembles or has a mannerism similar to someone who was mean to you as a child. I said earlier that I get anxious when furniture is moved in my home because, as a child, moving furniture always followed an argument between my parents.

We need to understand that our responses to current situations are often buried in classical and operant conditioning that may have happened years ago. For most of us, conflict was so often paired with unpleasant outcomes while we were growing up that we have become conditioned to fear it. It's no wonder that conflict, even at the lower levels of the conflict continuum, can trigger the fight or flight response!

Seductive power of punishment

Punishment is not a great tool for changing behavior because the changes it creates are not stable. While driving with two children in the back seat, you will probably hear something like, "He's touching me! Make him stop touching me!" Being the good parent, you might at first try reasoning with your children. However, when the behavior persists, you might lose patience and threaten punishment in a stern, no-nonsense voice, "Don't make me pull over!" You might then get silence for a few minutes, or, probably, just seconds. This silence rewards your threats because you got the desired result! However, the behavior soon returns. If you are like most, you increase the level of threat or you might even follow through with the threat. Once again, you are rewarded with the intended result, but for how long? It always comes back!

It is not uncommon for a supervisor to reprimand a direct report for not meeting an expectation. The supervisor has certainly gotten the direct report's attention and they might put in extra effort to achieve the expected standard. The supervisor is rewarded for using

94

punishment and is now more likely to use it again. The results can be devastating. The punishment has alerted the amygdala to danger and with that will come all the negative effects on thinking. Furthermore, the supervisor has, at least temporarily, damaged the relationship.

People will put in extraordinary effort to accomplish goals for a supervisor they trust and respect. On the other hand, they will do the minimum to get by when they don't trust or respect their supervisor. In addition, not wanting to put themselves at risk, they do the safe thing: they maintain the status quo, even when the problem requires a new or different approach.

There are two further issues which make punishment ineffective. The first is that, over time, people adapt to the punishment and it loses its effect. When this happens, you must increase the intensity of the punishment to get the desired effect. After a while it just becomes white noise when your supervisor regularly raises their voice and issues a lot of reprimands. To get a change in behavior the supervisor will have to increase the punishment. There comes a point when the supervisor runs out of tools to work with and dismissal is now on the table.

The other problem with punishment as a tool to change behavior is that it is only effective if the potential for punishment is present. "When the cat's away, the mice will play." Using punishment to influence behavior only works as long as the punisher is putting the pressure on. When the punisher lets up or is absent, the behavior will resort to previous levels.

Punishment as a tool for changing behavior is seductive. It rewards the punisher in the short-term. It gets immediate results but not the best results. Seeing the immediate change in behavior, the punisher is likely to resort to punishment again and again. In doing so, relationships are damaged. Quality employees leave or, feeling unappreciated or devalued, put less effort into their work. Alternatively, fearing for their job, they become stressed and the harder they try, the more mistakes they make. It's an ugly, downward spiral.

Generalizing from one event to other similar events

Stimulus generalization occurs when we learn something in one situation and apply it to other, similar situations. A big dog growls at you and chases you down the street. Now, all dogs, big or small, scare you. I avoid working with people in a specific office building because I have had three projects that went poorly in that building. I buy my coffee at any Starbucks because the staff in the Starbucks close to my home are always so friendly to me.

Customer service is all based on stimulus generalization – if you had a good interaction once, you will come back a second and a third time! This is the upside of stimulus generalization. In contrast, if you speak up in an inter-departmental meeting and feel like your input was disregarded, you might not contribute to future meetings, even when you are assured that folks would like to hear from you.

One-trial learning occurs when a punishing consequence, that is an unpleasant event, is severe enough. Get told once, "Maybe your next supervisor will appreciate your advice," and you are quite likely never to offer input to your boss again! The old adage applies: "fool me once, shame on you; fool me twice, shame on me!" It doesn't take a lot for a negative experience to shut down behavior in a whole lot of related situations!

Stimulus generalization can be either good or bad but, in conflict, it usually works against the individual's best interests. It is a major contributor to people's reluctance to deal with conflict directly.

If, for example, Janet has had several very difficult interactions with Amy and then she goes to a two-day workshop to learn new conflict management skills, it shouldn't be surprising that she is hesitant in using her new skills the next time she works with Amy. It takes a systematic plan to counter stimulus generalization when it is interfering with good outcomes. Providing Janet with the tools she would need is an essential start. This will need to be followed with some practice in a safe environment. Janet's supervisor or a colleague could help her to practice her new skills through role playing, using them to encourage her and providing increasingly difficult scenarios. Once Janet feels more comfortable, she could look for opportunities to contribute small comments in meetings where Amy is present. Small successes build quickly and, with a plan in action, stimulus generalization can be overcome.

Extinction

While stimulus generalization can be a problem, the situation is not dire. Extinction to the rescue! When a behavior has consistently been followed by a specific consequence, whether it be rewarding or punishing, the behavior becomes extinct if the sequence is disrupted. It simply disappears.

For example: little Sam wants a candy bar. Mom says no so Sam begins to whine and cry. Mom buys the candy bar. Guess what Sam does the next time they are in the checkout line in the candy store? This sequence is repeated, over and over. Sam knows exactly how to get Mom to buy the candy bar. If Mom wants the sequence to stop, she will need to stop rewarding the whining and crying with a candy bar. The first time she tries this, however, she is going to be confronted by the extinction burst. When we don't receive the expected reward for a previously rewarded behavior, we increase the intensity and duration of the behavior, and we might even add new behaviors to the sequence.

In this case, Mom tries to ignore the crying and whining and our little one cries louder and carries on and on, holds his breath, and throws things at Mom. Other shoppers are staring at her and maybe even shaking their heads. Mom feels this and she gives in to the extinction burst by buying the candy Sam wants. We are back to where we started, except that Sam has learned that a more intense version of his tantrum will be needed to get the candy. The next time they are in the grocery store, he will go straight to this more intense version to make sure he gets what he wants. If you can't weather the extinction burst, you shouldn't try using extinction to change a behavior. But, forewarned is forearmed and if you plan for the burst, extinction can undo bad behaviors.

Spontaneous recovery

While we are on the subject of being forewarned, we need to deal with the issue of spontaneous recovery. If you have successfully weathered the extinction burst and the unwanted behavior has disappeared, you need to know that it will come back, at least temporarily. Sam might not have a tantrum for a candy bar for several weeks and then, out of the blue, Mom is dealing with the tantrum again. This is a test to see if Mom's new response is real. If Mom resists the temptation to give in, just this once, the behavior will disappear for good. If she is tired or distracted and buys the candy bar, the old behavior will be back even stronger than it was before!

I would like to assure you that the extinction burst, and spontaneous recovery occurs only in children but that would be seriously misleading. If you start watching for it, you will see it everywhere.

Extinction in the workplace

So far, we have been talking about extinction as it applies to a child. What about at work? Xavier is a supervisor and works hard to support his staff. When they come to him with an issue, he goes to bat for them. Lately, it feels like he is always mediating issues between his staff and other areas. In the past, members of his team would occasionally need him to intercede, but the pattern has accelerated. Last week alone, most of his time was spent dealing with issues his staff should have handled. Wes, his best friend, pointed out the pattern. Staff members come to Xavier with a concern and, instead of helping them to solve their problems, he takes it on himself and rewards their complaints by relieving them of responsibility. Wes asked him, "If you are doing all the work, why do you have staff?" That really hit home for Xavier and, on Wes' advice, he decided to change things.

The next day Brooke came to him with a concern. Instead of offering to look into it, he asked Brooke a series of questions with the expectation that Brooke would solve her own problem. As expected, Brooke became frustrated. "Are you going to help me or not? I feel like you aren't listening." Wes warned him this might happen so he stayed the course, "I absolutely want to help you. That's why I'm asking questions – so you can see what your next step should be." This wasn't the response Brooke wanted and she got up to leave, "I can't believe you aren't helping me. Aren't you the supervisor? Aren't you supposed to help?" "You're right Brooke, I am supposed to help but I'm not going to do this for you. What I will do is help you to figure out how you can fix this yourself."

It wasn't easy but Xavier stayed firm, not only with Brooke but with all his team. Two weeks later Xavier found himself with a lot more time to do his own work and his team was doing a lot more of their own work. What was most interesting is that they seemed more committed to and proud of their work. He realized that his pattern of rescuing his team from difficult situations had inadvertently been undermining their confidence and creating unnecessary dependence.

Have you seen situations like this? Have you or someone you know been creating a dysfunctional pattern by reinforcing the wrong behavior? Extinction can reverse the pattern, but it will take some planning and a willingness to be strong in the face of pressure.

Applying conditioning to conflict

Not all conflicts at work need to be addressed directly. Many can be resolved by simply changing the reinforcement or punishment sequence. If a behavior is increasing, something is reinforcing it. If a behavior is decreasing, something is punishing it. It gets more complicated because rewards and punishers are not always obvious.

Devon was responsible for all the AV equipment for a large organization. If someone wanted access to the equipment, they had to go through Devon and he used this well. If you were nice to Devon, you got superb customer service. If Devon didn't like you, the equipment didn't show up when you needed it or it didn't work properly. Although Devon wasn't consciously aware of it, he was teaching people that they had better not get on his bad side.

Tom, Devon's supervisor, was getting complaints almost daily. Although he spoke to Devon about his pattern of behavior several times, Devon didn't change. Clearly Tom's reprimands couldn't compete with the experience of power Devon was feeling. Tom had several choices. He could reorganize his team so that Devon was no longer in control of the needed AV resources. Devon would certainly experience this as punishment which could prove to be counterproductive. Tom could begin a formal disciplinary process, but this too could be counterproductive. In many ways, Devon was a valuable employee. He worked hard, got a lot done, and, with his technical knowledge, he was an amazing problem-solver. Punishment could result in Devon leaving the organization or he might "quit and stay." The quitting and staying was a dynamic Tom didn't want to deal with.

A third option would be to look for samples of behavior that he could praise. Tom decided to put three pennies in his pocket and then, each day, deliberately look for behaviors he wanted from Devon. Every time Tom saw good customer service, he pointed it out to Devon and moved a penny to the other pocket. It didn't take very long before Devon was giving Tom more and more examples of the behavior he wanted. This is an example of "catching them doing the right thing" that Ken Blanchard has been teaching for over forty years.

Toolkit Summary

- Notice where conditioning may be the culprit in your or others' patterned behavior. If the same thing keeps happening, it may be a conditioned response.
- If you don't like the response you are getting, in yourself or others, change the consequence. Start rewarding the behavior you do want and stop rewarding the behavior you don't want.
- Avoid using punishment to change behavior. The change won't last and there are problematic side effects.
- Watch for stimulus generalization that may be shutting down a whole category of behavior. If you believe it is happening, put a systematic program of reinforcement in place to counter it.
- Use extinction to eliminate unwanted behavior. If you do, plan for the extinction burst and spontaneous recovery. Once you begin, you MUST stay the course.

9

Be Hypnotic!

Hypnosis and conflict

"Be hypnotic!" may seem like strange advice when dealing with conflict but it really isn't. Hollywood and stage shows have done a good job of raising awareness about hypnosis. Unfortunately, they have also done a good job of setting up myths and misunderstandings about what hypnosis is. When I tell folks that I am a certified hypnotherapist, I can usually expect to be asked if I will make them cluck like a chicken. While the question is asked in jest, there usually is some underlying concern. Hypnosis **is** about mind control. However, it's not the hypnotherapist who is doing the controlling, you are. All hypnosis is really self-hypnosis.

Hypnosis is a natural experience. You go in and out of hypnosis many, many times per day. I have a 50-minute commute to work and mid-point in my drive I cross a bridge over a large river. Often, I will notice where I am in my journey and know that I must have crossed the bridge, but I have no recall of doing so. I was in a trance, which is another word for hypnosis. Being in a trance simply means that I was engaged in selective focus. I was driving on autopilot while thinking

101

about something else. If something unusual occurred, I would easily snap out of my reverie and make any critical adjustments that might be necessary. For as long as things were predictable, however, I could focus my thoughts on something other than the road.

When I suggest that I was driving in a trance, it sounds quite dangerous because people don't understand what it really means. It is a natural occurrence and quite difficult to avoid. In fact, we need to learn to be "mindful" to take control of our daily trances. You shower in a trance. We often eat in a trance which, by the way, is one of the many contributors to obesity. We are in a trance when we read a book or watch T.V. It is easier to be in a trance than to not be in one. We go into and out of these automatic trances all day. The difference between these trances and the practice of hypnosis is that, with hypnosis, you take control of your mind and direct it to very specific, desired outcomes.

Hypnosis is a state in which we access our inner resources, the intuitive, creative parts of the mind. This can also lead to learning. Neurons communicate through electrical charges in the form of waves. These waves are measured in Hertz (Hz), which refers to the number of cycles per second. When you are alert and actively exerting mental energy, your brain demonstrates beta waves which cycle at 13Hz – 38Hz. The higher the number, the more energy is being exerted. When you are relaxed, you slip into alpha waves which cycle between 8-14Hz. The sweet spot for creativity is on the border between alpha and beta waves.

When you are in an alpha state, your conscious mind is subdued, and you are open to suggestion. You are also able to access resources deep within your subconscious, something you've already experienced many times. You go to bed troubled by a problem and wake up the next morning with an answer. Alternatively, you decide to take a break from the problem and go for a walk or listen to some music and, seemingly out of nowhere, an idea comes to you. When you create the conditions to slip into an alpha state, resources that were there all along bubble to the surface.

Mindful meditation has become very popular in the last few years and it is very similar to hypnosis. These two states are more similar than different in that they both involve focused attention and create deep relaxation by slowing the brain waves. Mindfulness is focused on being in the moment and accepting one's feelings, thoughts, and sensations with the goal of releasing negativity and judgement. Hypnosis seeks to recruit the subconscious to the task of forming new responses, thoughts, attitudes, behaviors, or feelings.

Guided visualizations and progressive relaxation, autogenic training, and neuro-linguistic programming are all subsets or close cousins of hypnosis. They can all be very useful in preparing for a difficult conversation. They are excellent tools for releasing stress which will then help you to think more clearly, stay calm when in the conversation, and hear the other party's perspective. At the very least, your body language will naturally be less threatening, resulting in less defensiveness in the other party. You can also use these tools proactively to lower your overall reactivity to daily events. Even a few minutes a day will make a difference.

When you are in a state of hypnosis, you are not asleep, but you are deeply relaxed. The brain cannot be relaxed and anxious simultaneously so through hypnosis, you can let the past be the past and be free from worry about the future. This is very important for dealing with conflict.

Earlier on, I said that you can't just decide to feel differently about something. Feelings belong to the emotional brain and cannot be controlled by the conscious mind. When we are in hypnosis, however, we have calmed the conscious mind, our critical faculty, and are accessing our subconscious mind. This is how we get our elephant, our subconscious mind, to cooperate with the conscious brain. Under hypnosis, we can set an intention regarding how we would like to respond to situations. We can also reset our beliefs to free ourselves from those that have been limiting our achievements or preventing us from achieving desired changes.

To help you get ready for your conversation, I have provided you with a self-hypnosis session that you can download at: https://conflictatworkbook.com/resources/. Listen to this session at least once, more if you have the time, prior to a difficult conversation and you will it will help you to stay calm and think more clearly when you are holding the conversation.

Irrational beliefs and conflict

As we grow up, our parents, schools, coaches, media, and culture teach us and reinforce specific ideas about how the world works. We don't question these beliefs which continue to mediate our relationships with the world, guide our decisions and behaviors, and dictate our emotions. Albert Ellis, the father of Rational Emotive Behavior Therapy (REBT), argued that we all suffer from three musts: "I must do well; you must treat me well; and the world must be easy." Out of these three musts, irrational beliefs emerge.

Our acceptance of irrational beliefs causes much of our conflict and suffering, which would dissipate if we challenged these beliefs. Letting go of these beliefs would mean that we are no longer hurt, disappointed, or frustrated when others do not behave according to our irrational expectations. Letting go would also change some of our own behavior and this might produce less friction in our relationships.

The following is a list of the most common irrational beliefs. If you are curious, you can go to *http://www.testandcalc.com/Self_Defeating_Beliefs/questtxt.asp* and take a short assessment to help you identify which irrational beliefs are causing you the most angst.

1. *I need love and approval from those significant to me, and I must avoid disapproval from any source.*

    It is unlikely than anyone would ever unconditionally approve of everything you do.

2. *To feel happy and worthwhile, I must achieve, succeed at whatever I do, and make no mistakes.*

    No one is competent in all things or at all times. Total security and absolute perfection does not exist. The search of unattainable perfection is a major energy drain.

3. *People should always do the right thing. When they behave obnoxiously, unfairly, or selfishly, they must be blamed and punished.*

    People can make mistakes without realizing it. These mistakes are not consciously evil. People do things without thinking through the impact their actions have on others.

4. *Things must be the way I want them to be; otherwise, life will be intolerable.*

   Events are determined by a variety of factors, many of which we cannot control.

5. *My unhappiness is caused by things outside of my control, so there is little I can do to feel any better.*

   We may not have control over the things that affect us, but we do have control over how we respond to them. Things will only affect us to the extent that we allow them to and according to the meaning we attach to them.

6. *I must worry about things that could be dangerous, unpleasant, or frightening; otherwise, they might happen.*

   Worrying about things robs the present of happiness. Obsessing over something makes it worse. Being anxious prevents us from dealing effectively with stressful or dangerous events.

7. *I can be happier by avoiding life's difficulties, unpleasantness and responsibilities.*

   Avoiding things makes it worse in two ways. The weight of the deferred tasks drains our energy and, by deferring them, tasks often get bigger.

8. *We absolutely need someone stronger or greater than ourselves to rely on.*

   When we depend on others, we make fewer choices for ourselves and we limit our opportunities to learn. This creates a cycle of further dependence and insecurity.

9. *Events in my past are causing my problems and they continue to influence my feelings and behaviors now.*

   While the past can serve as an important lesson for the future it cannot become an excuse for not making the personal effort which is necessary to move forward.

10. *I should become upset when other people have problems and feel unhappy when they are sad.*

Solving problems for others does not help them to grow and it creates dependence. As part of a community, we do have some altruistic obligations, but this must be balanced with the responsibility of helping people to become self-sufficient. Feeling sad because others are struggling does nothing to help the situation.

11. *I shouldn't have to feel discomfort and pain. I can't stand them and must avoid them at all cost.*

Growth comes through challenge and, with growth, comes a sense of control and increased self-esteem.

12. *Every problem should have an ideal solution, and it is intolerable when one can't be found.*

Some problems are highly complex and cannot be solved in the short term.

You probably don't have to take the assessment to know which of the above irrational beliefs might be causing you the most stress. If we are being honest with ourselves, we can usually identify these patterns of thought. Once we know what they are, we can challenge them and, over time, we can rewire our brain. This is the long way. It's like taking old two-lane roads to travel across the country. It can be done but these roads meander, have lots of stops and, if you get behind a farmer's tractor, you could be slowed down for miles. When I have a distance to travel, I prefer taking a four-lane highway.

Hypnosis is that four-lane highway if you want to replace irrational beliefs with a new and more functional pattern that will serve you better. To help you chase away irrational beliefs, you can go to https://conflictatworkbook.com/resources/ and download a self-hypnosis recording. Listen to the recording often and you will be less bothered by any irrational beliefs that are currently getting in your way.

When dealing with a difficult conversation, knowledge of the three musts and irrational beliefs can also guide you in understanding the underlying response you are seeing in others. Fear is always at the root of any conflict and you can make an educated guess as to which of these irrational beliefs might be sparking the other person's fear. This knowledge could help you create some safety for this person.

For example, Rodney puts a lot of pressure on himself to get things right the first time. Perfection is not possible, and things don't always happen the way Rodney planned. Rodney reacted poorly when Tony asked him to re-work an assignment. He didn't give Tony a chance to explain what the issue was or how it could be fixed. Instead, he muttered something under his breath, left Tony's office, and then threw the file down on his desk with such force that several folks looked up to see what had happened.

Rodney's need to be perfect had blocked an opportunity to learn and, more importantly, impacted negatively on his relationship with Tony and his co-workers. People who pursue perfection fear that they are not worthwhile. Anything short of perfection sets them up for rejection. Pointing out Rodney's success on a previous task, or what part of the present task was good, might have helped Rodney to hear that his work did have value. At the very least, although the behavior would still have been unacceptable, understanding the source of Rodney's reactions might have prevented the tension from escalating.

Influence and hypnosis

Hollywood has made it seem as though one could hypnotize others without their knowledge and then you could control their behavior. If that were possible, I wouldn't be spending my time writing; I would be out there hypnotizing folks to pay my bills for me! Hypnosis does not magically give you power over someone else. At best, hypnosis can be used to influence the other party's willingness to change their response towards you. In an earlier chapter we discussed the use of language. Words such as *'imagine'* or *'I wonder'* help the other party to visualize a different outcome. As a result, they might be more motivated towards changing a behavior.

We also discussed the principle of reciprocity and the how it could influence a person's behavior. Robert Cialdini, in his book, *Influence: The Psychology of Persuasion,* provides six principles that influence behavior:

- Reciprocity – people expect to repay in kind;
- Scarcity – people want what is not readily available;
- Social proof (consensus) – people follow the lead of similar others;

- Authority – people defer to experts or people in charge;
- Consistency or commitment – people act in ways that demonstrates personal alignment. They tend to fulfill written, public and voluntary commitments.
- Liking – people will cooperate with others who are similar to themselves or who demonstrate that they respect or care about them.

Although Cialdini wouldn't describe these principles as tools for hypnosis, they do serve to alter a person's focus. People change their behavior without being consciously aware of the principles which influenced the change. In most cases, their conscious brain would argue that they themselves chose to act in the way they did.

When I first read Cialdini's book, I was fascinated with these six principles. As it happened, I was in the market to buy a new car. These principles are commonly used to sell cars, so I made a little cheat sheet on which I listed them. I thought this would help me to avoid paying too much for the car. It didn't work! Even though I could identify each time the salesperson put one of these principles into action, they were so powerful that I couldn't help myself and I paid $2,000 more for the car than I had planned. This was self-hypnosis in action. I was so focused on how much I loved the car, how nice the sales person was, and how I was going to feel when I drove the car to work the next day, that details slipped past me and I ended up signing a contract that included lots of little extras.

I am not suggesting that you should use these principles in the same way that the salesperson did to get me to pay too much for a car. It isn't ethical. I used this example to illustrate just how powerful these principles can be. Whether you use them consciously or not, these principles are a part of almost every interaction with another person. When there is a conflict, it is worth looking at which of these principles are influencing the interaction and whether they are helping or hindering the outcome. A simple thing like reminding the other person that you care about them, if you honestly do, can go a long way towards reducing tension. Recognizing the value of the other party's expertise on a project can improve a person's willingness to collaborate.

These principles offer such a wealth of opportunity to easily resolve problems between people that it is worth our while to try to understand and use them.

Toolkit Summary

- We go in and out of a trance many times a day.
- These trances can be used to access inner resources.
- Mindful meditation, guided visualization, progressive relaxation, neurolinguistic programming, and self-hypnosis are similar in that they can all be used to relieve stress and to access a resourceful state.
- You can use any of these tools proactively to reduce your reactivity to daily events.
- You can also use any of these tools to create calmness in preparation for a difficult conversation.
- Everyone acquires some irrational beliefs and these beliefs can cause unnecessary suffering.
- You can identify which irrational beliefs are affecting you negatively and use self-hypnosis to free yourself from them.
- Knowing the underlying irrational beliefs in a conflict situation can help you to adjust your behavior to minimize their effect.
- Cialdini's six principles of influence change behavior at a subconscious level.
- These principles of influence are a part of every interaction and can be used to reduce tension in a conflict.

10

Aiki Breakthrough Change Method

" Help, please" was the opening line on Jacob's email. "I'm between a rock and a hard place, can I stop by this afternoon?" was the rest of the message. "Of course, I'm open any time after 3," was my reply.

When Jacob arrived, he looked worn out. "Tell me, what's going on?" I asked him.

He responded, "Taylor has told me to hold some information back on a report I am preparing. If I do that, I will be in violation of company policy."

Taylor, Jacob's supervisor, had run into some trouble with the CEO the previous month, and I could guess that the information he wanted held back was just going to deepen his problems. Even knowing this, I was concerned that perhaps Jacob was overreacting.

"How do you know that holding back that information would violate company policy?" I asked.

"I confirmed it with Taylor. I asked him, 'Are you sure you want me to write the report that way?' I even reminded him that holding back critical information would violate our integrity code. He said he didn't care about the integrity code and that he didn't want the information shared. So, I followed up with an email asking him to confirm that he wanted the information held back and he never answered."

"Are you concerned that if you do as he tells you to and anyone finds out, you will be held accountable?" I asked.

"Yes," he replied emphatically. "Last year he made me do something which I knew was against policy. I got written up for it and he denied telling me to do it. If I don't do as he says, he will write me up for insubordination! I just can't win on this one."

Are you stuck?

Some conflicts feel as though there is just no way out. Have you ever been in a situation like Jacob's? When you feel caught up in an either/or dilemma and neither direction is good, the world can look very bleak. Perhaps your situation is not quite like Jacob's but one in which it feels as though the conflict is so big that you just don't know where to start. Or, maybe, the conflict has been going on for years and you have tried everything you can think of and you just can't resolve it. Sometimes you might think that you have fixed a conflict and then it rears its ugly head again, when you least expect it. At other times, it feels as though the problem just can't be fixed, and you resign yourself to accepting a bad situation.

If you are experiencing any of these scenarios, it's time for a radically different approach. That's where the Aiki Breakthrough Change (ABC) method can help.

Doing the wrong thing and thinking it's right

When a new driver or a driver new to northern weather finds their car stuck in snow, they do exactly the wrong thing and they rev their motor. Intuitively it makes sense that if you are stuck you should just give the car more gas and then, with the extra energy, you will get a grip and be able to move your car. The problem with this approach is that it is exactly the wrong thing to do. What you are in fact doing when you rev your engine in the snow is digging the wheels deeper into the snow. At the same time, you are also heating things up just enough to create a film of moisture that immediately freezes. Now, you're deeper into the snow and you are trying to get a grip on ice. That just doesn't work!

The same thing happens when we are stuck in a conflict. We try, and try, and try, if not in actual behavior, at least in our head. We rev our brains trying to find a solution and, just as it doesn't work well in the snow, it isn't getting us anywhere with our conflict. If anything, we are digging ourselves deeper and deeper. When you are struggling with a conflict that feels bigger than you are, you may begin to ruminate on it. You try to let it go but you find your mind wandering back to it, repeatedly. As time passes, you get angrier or more depressed, or both. That feeling of helplessness begins to color everything and robs you of the pleasure that you might otherwise feel in other activities. This is no way to live.

When you are in this "stuck" phase, a well-meaning friend might offer some ideas or invite you to brainstorm solutions. You might respond with an exasperated, "Yes, but…" to their ideas or with a list of all the things you have tried already. Or you might explain to the friend all the things which you have thought of trying and why they won't work. It's time to change your focus because staring at the problem is not moving you forward.

The Aiki tool provides a way to break through the spinning wheels in your mind and make change easy. With this tool, you can recruit both the conscious and subconscious brain and, when you do this, it's like taking the super-highway to your destination instead of the less direct and slower two-lane road. The Aiki approach allows the subconscious mind, with all its creativity, to be fully engaged in the problem-solving process while lulling the conscious brain into seeing the entire exercise as a fun game.

The science behind doing the wrong thing

When you persistently fail in your effort to achieve a goal or resolve a conflict, you begin to believe that you have no control over the situation. Once this is how you feel, you will probably give up on any further effort. After all, what's the point? You are trapped and no amount of effort will change that situation. Your self-efficacy is trickling away. Have you ever felt like this?

When you reach this state it almost feels as though you have forgotten, or maybe never knew, how to help yourself. In Chapter 4, I explained that the functions of the hippocampus include managing short-term memory and learning, and also turning off the stress response. These functions are eroded when the hippocampus is continually exposed to high levels of cortisol. When you are dealing with a problem or a conflict that you just can't break through, your fight-or-flight response is constantly engaged and your ability to think about new solutions has been marginalized. Worse, you are not able to turn off the cortisol by slowing the fight-or-flight response. In fact, you are dumbed down!

The emotional brain, already activated by the desire to make something unpleasant go away, notes the lack of success. Fear that the problem will not be resolved starts to set in. The problem grows in the person's mind. It's getting bigger and, with each new solution attempted, the belief that the problem is unsolvable grows stronger. This further reduces the person's ability to effectively execute another strategy, offering even more evidence that the situation is hopeless and that they are helpless in effecting the desired change. In Jacob's case, his memory of how poorly this same situation turned out in the past adds to his sense of helplessness and hopelessness. It's easy to see how this is creating a downward spiral to despair.

The standard approach of asking you what change you would like or how you would like to feel instead of the way you are currently feeling just feeds the current "stuck" situation. These questions will just remind you that you are not in control and the probability of your being able to answer with anything that will be useful to the situation is pretty low.

Hebb's Law and Long-Term Potentiation (LTP) come into play when trying to guide a person to make changes while they are in this "stuck" state. When a neuron fires and neurotransmitters travel to a second neuron, that neuron might also fire but something extra happens. The second neuron opens neurotransmitter receptors that were previously closed, and this then makes the second neuron more sensitive to the firing of the first neuron. It's as if the second neuron is expecting a further signal from the first neuron. This is the phenomenon of LTP

(Carson & Tiers, 2014)[11]. With repetition, this expectancy becomes cemented and according to Hebb's Law, neurons that fire together, become wired together.

Applying this to Jacob, the more he pays attention to his feelings of helplessness and views his situation as out of his control and unsolvable, the more the problem persists. The frequently cited quote from Henry Ford, "Whether you think you can, or you think you can't…you're right" sadly applies perfectly to this situation. When we ask Jacob what change he does want or how he would like to think or feel differently, we are just refocusing him on his problem state in the same way that he himself has been focusing on it. As he attempts to focus on a different future, it fires the program in his head which tells him that he has failed several times in the past. Any action that is initiated under these conditions has a high probability of meeting the same fate as all his previous attempts at change. The difference is that now Jacob has additional evidence that the situation is hopeless!

The way out of this downward spiral is to interrupt the pattern. We can't reinforce the existing pattern if we want to help the person who is defining themselves as a victim or helpless; we must do something differently.

Aiki philosophy

Years ago, I attended an Aikido demonstration with my son who was then seven years old. I watched in awe as my little boy flipped a six-foot man after just a few minutes of instruction. I asked the instructor how this could be possible, and he explained that in the Aikido marshal art, it's all about leverage, taking control of your opponent's energy and re-directing it for you own purpose. It seemed to me that this approach could be applied to persistent problems in the same way.

Aikido, which is often translated as "the way of harmony" is a relatively new martial art that has only defensive moves. Developed in Japan around 1920 by Morihei Ueshiba, the purpose of Aikido is to provide the practitioner with a method of defending themselves without harming the aggressor. The word "aikido" is formed of three kanji:

合 – ai – joining, unifying, combining, fitting

気 – ki – spirit, energy, mood, morale

道 – dō – way, path

Most physical or verbal conflict is linear in its attack. The aggressor moves directly towards the target. The target's natural response to either a physical or a verbal attack is to defend themselves or to push back against the aggressor. The proverbial fight-or-flight response is activated in the target who then resists/fights or escapes/flees. When the target's response to the attack does not get the desired result, the subconscious or emotional brain, which is already activated by the fight-or-flight response, takes note and increases the intensity of its fight-or-flight. It also begins to question whether the situation can be stabilized, and fear grows.

The aggressor and the target are now in a downward spiraling dance. In response to the target's fight-or-flight response the aggressor escalates its energy towards the target. This clash of responses continues the downward spiral of anger and fear and both participants in this dance suffer harm. Regardless of whether it is a physical or a verbal attack, the aggressor's determination for dominance is fueled by a sense of alienation from the target. Losing ground to the target will represent proof of failure and loss of standing in, or respect from, their peer group. A similar dynamic is operating for the target. Pushing back and coming out of the altercation as the victor is critical to self-identity, self-esteem, and acceptance within the tribe. Loss aversion, our drive to hold on to what we have and to not allow others to take what we see as ours adds to the downward spiral as we slip further and further away from connection to the other person. The violence, both real and symbolic, escalates. Neither side will come out of this situation whole.

The Aikido approach for responding to conflict seeks to harmonize with the attacker and to resolve the situation without either party being harmed. It does this by converting the linear motion of the attack into a circular flow of energy and thereby flipping its direction. In doing so, the practitioner of Aikido takes control and uses the attacker's energy for their own purpose. By joining with the attacker instead of confronting them, the energy is now working in the target's favor and against the attacker.

Applying the Aiki philosophy to interpersonal conflict

We can use the Aikido philosophy as a metaphor for gaining a better understanding of Jacob's situation. With this better understanding, those in a similar situation can be guided toward a better result. Jacob was focused on what he didn't want. He was taking a linear, direct approach to make what he didn't want to go away. Given what he didn't want, he implemented what should have been a solution; he tried to talk Taylor out of holding back information. The solution he tried didn't make the issue go away and he invested more energy into fighting the problem or finding ways to avoid the problem. In Jacob's case, he sent me an urgent email for help.

Using an Aiki approach, we can do something differently. While we focus on a problem, including all its pain and frustration, all our energy is usually being spent on finding an escape. With the Aiki approach, rather than escaping, the individual is asked to lean into the problem. This is decidedly counter-intuitive. It takes the energy that is currently focused on the problem but instead of working to escape the problem, it is accepted. The Aiki approach even prescribes that more energy resources should be devoted to the problem but now, in a different direction.

When my boys were young, to register their protest and to show me that they were in control, they each attempted slamming a door or stomping up the stairs. My response was to take control of the situation by insisting that if they were going to slam a door or stomp up the stairs, they needed to do it right. I would then make them practice the behavior several times. My response took the power away from the behavior. Clearly, they were not in control, I was! It was also funny, and they would end up laughing as they repeated the behavior. More importantly, they didn't slam a door or stomp up the stairs the next time they were upset with me. This was an Aiki move!

With the Aiki approach, instead of escaping the problem, you are encouraged to think about stabilizing it at its current level or even increasing it. This is reminiscent of the "prescribing the symptom" which was introduced by the famed hypnotist and therapist, Milton Erickson. Erickson had the client engage in the very behavior they wanted help in eliminating, but they engaged in it with a small difference - they were now supposed to engage in the behavior. This small difference made all the difference. Milton Erickson pointed out that a small hole in a dam would weaken the entire structure and being required to engage in the very behavior they were trying to change was the small hole.

This is the key to the Aiki approach. It invites the person to engage in the very outcome they are trying to change. Instead of devoting energy to escaping the situation, the energy is now redirected towards immersing in the challenge. Instead of using energy to reduce or eliminate the problem, the energy is being used to figure out how to make the challenge bigger.

With Aiki, the individual is asked, "What are all the actions or strategies you can put into play to ensure that [*the problem*] never improves or even gets worse?" When confronted with this question, the individual is invariably taken aback. The question often needs to be repeated. It is exactly opposite to what they thought you would ask. This counter-intuitive perspective jolts their thinking and serves as the pattern interrupt which forces them to think about their challenge in a completely different way. It is common to get a laugh when the question is repeated and the brainstorming that follows is frequently done tongue-in-cheek. That works because they are now throwing out all kinds of unedited, "crazy" ideas.

In most cases, the individual's subconscious really does know what is needed. The conscious, rational, logical brain steps aside when you pose the Aiki question because the question is **not** logical or rational. The act of brainstorming about how to make a problem remain the same or get worse is totally opposite to what the individual wants, and therefore, the exercise is not taken seriously – it's goofy. The conscious, logical, rational brain can step aside because its services are just not needed!

Truth telling can now surface. Within the list of brainstormed ideas are some actions that have been contributing towards maintaining the problem. That individual had not previously admitted to themselves that these actions played a role in causing the problem or they had simply been completely unaware of it. As a result of brainstorming the Aiki question, the thought is out there. It's been verbalized and has usually been written down on paper. There is an ah-ha moment and following this the path forward is now clear. Reverse one or more of the actions that are maintaining the problem and the situation will change dramatically.

Steps of the Aiki approach

1. Identify the actual conflict you want resolved. Explain it in detail so that you are very clear what it is you really want as an outcome. It's easy to get confused and focus only on a symptom of the bigger problem. In Jacob's case, he could be thinking he wants his boss to let him put the complete information in the report. What Jacob really wants is a relationship with his boss that is based on mutual respect and trust.

2. Write down at least ten things you could do to ensure that you will not achieve or have what you really want. Be creative and go well beyond ten if the ideas are coming easily. In Jacob's case, one idea might be to simply quit his job.

3. Once you have your ideas written down, look them over carefully and identify which of these things you are already doing. Place a check mark beside them. This is a time for complete honesty. When you are struggling with an ongoing conflict or one that feels too big to even begin to address, you will often discover, if you are being truly honest with yourself, that you are engaging in some counter-productive behaviors.

4. Create a plan to change those behaviors which you now recognize as having contributed to the problem.

5. Review the list again to see if there are any items that you might be able to reverse. One item on Jacob's list was, "Never engage in any small talk with Taylor." Jacob realized that he and Taylor were virtually strangers to each other. Their only relationship was their work relationship. It's hard to build trust when you don't really know someone. Small talk won't solve the whole problem, but it could bring a solution one step closer. Add this one small step to a couple of other steps, and you could make some progress.

6. Execute the plan! Once you've identified what you could do differently, it isn't worth the paper it's written on if you don't act. Monitor your progress as you implement your plan and, if necessary, adjust or repeat the process. Above all, don't give up!

Toolkit Summary

- When we are stuck, we often do exactly the wrong thing and think it's right.
- When we are in fight-or-flight mode, we tend to focus our energy on escaping the problem.
- The Aiki approach redirects the energy toward the problem and engages the subconscious. It encourages you to think about the problem very differently: "How can I ensure that [*the problem*] never improves."
- Implement the six Aiki steps and you might discover behaviors that are currently getting in the way and new behaviors that can move you closer to resolving the conflict.

11

The CLEAN/N Model

The CLEAN/N conversation

Sue burst into my office, obviously distraught. "I need your help. I think I'm going to get fired and it just isn't fair."

"Tell me what's going on," I said.

"My boss used to have my job and she thinks she knows what it takes to do the work but there have been so many changes in the rules and regulations that even the simplest of tasks take twice as long as when I first started working here. On top of that, the consulting firm HR hired has put a performance evaluation system in place that requires every statement to be documented with three supporting observations. I have eight direct-reports and each evaluation is taking thirty hours and I am way behind in my work."

"Have you talked with Beth about your workload?" I asked.

"I tried. Last week I missed letting Beth know about an important meeting and she was really angry. When I explained about my workload, Beth said that she didn't have time for excuses and things falling off the radar. She said she was going to work with me over the next week because missing deadlines is not an option. I think the only reason she is working with me is so that she can get more evidence to fire me. I'm working until 7 p.m. every night but I never seem to catch up."

Has anything like this ever happened to you? You are in a situation in which it feels like the harder you try to do the right thing, the worse things seem to get? Many conversations on the conflict continuum can be avoided, minimized, or easily resolved by using the tools we have discussed so far: improving our mindset, using a kindness approach, avoiding triggers and sprinkling in sparks, attending to body language, make conditioning work for us instead of against us, using self-hypnosis, storytelling and finally, considering principles that influence behavior.

All these tools can be used at the lower end of the conflict continuum. However, when a conflict has reached the level of discord or dispute, a systematic strategy for holding a conversation needs to be added to the conflict management plan. The CLEAN/N conversation provides that vehicle and this is what I advised Sue to use. The acronym stands for: **C**an we talk; **L**ist the facts; **E**xplain your meaning; **A**sk for their meaning; **N**eutralize or **N**ext Steps.

"This is a tough spot to be in, Sue. You might be right about Beth's intentions or there might be something else going on," I commented.

"No, there's nothing else going on. She's out to get me!"

When we are in a difficult situation like this, it's hard to let go of our first interpretation of the situation. We are meaning-makers and we are wired to protect ourselves, which means we are going to go to the "dark side" first. Our meaning makes sense to us and it is hard to let it go but, if we want to truly move to a good result, we need to be open to the possibility that there **could** be another meaning that also fits the facts. If you are like me, there have been situations when you were sure you knew what was going on and you took action based on that knowledge, only to discover that there was more to the story. More than once I said or did something that I had to apologize for once the rest of the story emerged. This is a good prescription for damaging relationships.

121

I asked Sue, "What do you want? Do you want Beth to just leave you alone or do you want a better working relationship with Beth?"

"I want Beth to understand what I am up against and to help me. I can't keep working these extra hours, but I really need this job. When I first started here, I really loved the work. I still do, but now there's just too much of it!"

"OK then, you're going to have to talk with Beth. Let's walk through the steps of a CLEAN/N conversation."

Step 1: Can we talk

"First, you are going to have to set up the conversation. A critical first step is asking permission. These kinds of conversations always feel a little threatening to both parties. By asking permission, it gives Beth some feeling of control. A basic human drive is to maintain control because with control comes predictability. When we can anticipate what is about to happen, we can take proactive steps to protect ourselves. This reduces our sense of vulnerability and most importantly, the sense of threat. The conversation is going to be much more productive if threat levels for both of you are at a minimum.

Another reason why asking for permission is important is because it might truly not be a good time to have the discussion. If Beth has a meeting in five minutes, feels the location for the discussion is not right for any reason, or is in the middle of meeting a critical deadline, the conversation will be resented, rushed or given very little attention. Feeling pressured by the clock, uncomfortable with the location or busy dealing with other demands is not a good prescription for positive results.

Finally, asking permission to have the conversation is a good tool for gauging Beth's emotional temperature. If you get permission, you are free to move on to the next step. If, instead, you get a no; a hesitant, deer-in-the-headlights response; or a yes, that really sounds more like a no; then, you need to hit the pause button and create safety.

If you proceed without getting safety, nothing good is going to happen. You cannot hold a productive, rational conversation when either party is in fight or flight mode. When the amygdala sounds the alarm and the stress response has been activated, the quality of thinking is eroded and automatic and habitual responses are in full swing. We are literally 'dumbed' down in this condition and getting to a creative solution to a problem becomes highly unlikely."

Creating safety to de-escalate the conflict

"If Beth appears to be stressed, how do I create safety?"

"The good news for you is that you have choices. You can show that you care, you can apologize if there is something to apologize for, you can establish mutual purpose, or you can use a contrast tool."

Showing you care:

The most effective way to create safety is to express genuine caring for the other party. Notice the word *genuine*. If you don't really care about the other person and you suggest that you do, your body language will give you away. There are many "tells" in your body language that you cannot consciously control and which the other party will read at a subconscious level. Without being able to say exactly why, the other party will know if your words don't match your heart. That disconnect between your words and your body language will create mistrust and further increase the other party's sense of threat.

Expressing genuine caring for another person can be as simple as telling them that you respect them or the work they do. Or, you might say something like, "I like working with you and I want us to get back to being comfortable with each other again." *If you feel it, find a way to say it.* Knowing someone likes you, is almost irresistible. If I understand that you care about me, my need to defend myself against you dissipates. Friends look out for each other; that's what friends do! On a physical level, expressing caring for the other person stimulates a surge of oxytocin in both parties which results in a feeling of connection and well-being. Expressing caring may not be enough to make the conversation easy, but it will certainly improve the likelihood of being able to have a rational discussion.

Apologize if an apology is warranted.

Apologizing for something over which you had no control is empty, disingenuous, and counterproductive. Your body language will give you away if you don't really mean the apology. However, if you

123

recognize that there was something you did that caused harm or hurt, then an apology is in order. A good apology will specify exactly what you are apologizing for. A simple "I'm sorry" or "I apologize" doesn't work because the other party is left guessing what you are apologizing for. The lack of effort involved in throwing out two words truly undermines the effect. Finish the sentence with the specifics and then add some commitment regarding future behavior. For example, "I'm sorry I was so abrupt this morning. When you have a concern, you deserve my full attention."

If you make an excuse for your behavior when you apologize, it doesn't sound like you really meant the apology. The word "but" is going to negate anything that came before it! There are times when an explanation feels important and, if you add the commitment for changed behavior, the excuse will not have the same negative effect on the apology. Using the previous example, you might say, "I'm sorry I was abrupt this morning. I was working with a deadline, but you deserve my full attention and I will do better the next time." As the listener, I now understand what the context was. I also understand that you are not letting yourself off the hook and you intend to behave differently in the future.

Shared purpose:

When we are in the middle of a dispute or open discord, we tend to see the other party as the "enemy"; they are not part of our tribe. This separateness can be mitigated by reminding ourselves and the other party that we have a shared goal, a mutual purpose. Saying something like, "We both want this project to succeed" or "I know you care as much about the organization as I do" helps to change the perspective. It's difficult to have a meaningful conversation when you are separated by a wall. Clarifying our shared purpose helps to move both parties to the same side of the wall. This is a better starting point for a healthy conversation.

Using a contrast statement:

This is a tool that comes from *Crucial Conversations* and is based on the premise that it isn't what you are saying that causes resistance. It's what the other person **thinks** you are saying.

For example, Marie and Bob have scheduled a meeting to discuss a project and how to fund it. Bob's history with budget discussions with others has been contentious. When Marie schedules the meeting, Bob believes she intends to pressure him into giving up budget dollars for the project. This suspicion about her intention is in the room and whether it is openly discussed or not, it will affect his responses to anything Marie has to say. However, if Marie uses a contrast statement, "I'm not here to talk about your budget; I just want to talk through ideas you might have about how a project like this could be funded" she can create a different base for their discussion.

A contrast statement has two parts: firstly, what your intention is **not** and secondly, what your intention **is**. The contrast statement eliminates the guess work. It allows the other party to release any fears and to refocus their attention on what needs to be resolved. To construct a contrast statement, you need to make an educated guess about what the other person might be assuming your intention is and then clearly deny it. You then follow up with a clear statement of what you do intend to achieve.

A statement such as: "I don't want you to think I don't appreciate your efforts; although we do need to talk about some of the details in this report," can be made even stronger by slipping in an assurance between the first half and the second half of the statement. It might be worded this way: "I don't want you to think I don't appreciate your efforts because I have seen the extra hours you have put in and I know you really care about this project. We do need to talk about some of the details in this report." Contrast statements take a little practice but once you have them mastered, they are a very effective tool for increasing the other person's sense of safety.

I explained to Sue, "If you were to use a contrast statement with Beth, you might say something like, "'I don't want you to think that I don't want your help *[not your intention]*. The work has changed since you had this job and I could really use your insight as to how to manage the workload *[expressing respect and assurance – not an essential part of the contrast statement but it helps]*. I would like an opportunity to share with you just how much the work has changed because I'm not sure just what I am dealing with. Can we talk about *[my intention]*?"

"Let me write that down so I can remember it," Sue responded.

Step 2: List the facts.

"The next step is to list your facts for Beth, " I explained. "Remember, a fact is something that is true. It is consistent with objective reality and it can be verified. When you list the facts for Beth, you create an objective base of agreement. For example, 'Your workday starts at 8 am; you arrived after 8 am three times last week.' Either you were here on time or you were not!"

Listing the facts does not mean listing every fact. There are going to be many facts in any dispute. You pick out the most relevant facts and you share them with the other party. If you are upset about something, just taking the time to step back and think about what the actual facts are can change your perspective and your feelings about the situation. It takes work to sift through a situation and to identify the most relevant facts. When you do, you can paint a concise picture of the situation for yourself and for the other party.

Most difficult conversations miss this step of listing facts and move directly to the next step: explain your meaning, which is the subjective interpretation of the event. Your interpretation may or may not be accurate but, regardless, it is unlikely that the other party shares the same interpretation. It is these differences in understanding or interpretation that can cause major mistrust and misunderstanding. Start with the facts because they did or didn't happen. The objectivity of facts allows you to set a base of common understanding. The other party may have some additional facts to add to the mix but once again, it's a fact or it isn't. Sharing your facts is the first step towards understanding and agreement.

"What are the facts of this situation, Sue?" I prompted.

Counting them off on her fingers, she said "One, Beth once had my job. Two, new regulations and process changes have made the work more complicated. Three, the HR performance evaluations have been taking up most of my time for the last few weeks. Four, I missed telling Beth about an important meeting. Five, I am behind on several projects and in danger of missing some deadlines." Sue moves to her other hand, "Six, Beth wants to work with me next week, and seven, Beth is collecting evidence to fire me."

"You did great until you got to number seven, Sue. Is that really a fact?" I commented.

"Maybe not but it sure feels like a fact!" Sue emphasized.

"Yeah, meanings you attach to facts usually do," I reminded her.

Step 3: Explain your meaning.

"After you have listed these facts, it's time to explain to Beth what you are thinking. This Is where your seventh point comes in to play. It fits here, in this step."

"You mean, I just tell her I think she is trying to fire me?" Sue asked.

"If you share your facts first, Beth can now see why you came to your conclusion. She can see the logic even though it isn't comfortable for either of you. Whether you say it or not, Beth can figure out what you're thinking. By putting it out there and just saying it, you can both deal with it."

As a species, we are meaning-makers. Something happens and our minds immediately scan for a similar pattern from the past and attach the new event onto that pattern. Our mind is constantly judging: good/bad; safe/dangerous; like/dislike. If Adele comes to a meeting without the right file, you attach a label to the event: disorganized or doesn't care about doing a good job. If Ronnie surprises you by bringing you a cup of coffee, you might label that event: kind, thoughtful, cares about me. We are always judging, and it happens so fast that the meaning we attach to an event – the label – gets mixed in with the facts. We easily lose sight of what the facts are and the additional meaning which we have attached to the facts. They become one in our memory and that's what sets off the downward spiral in many difficult conversations.

Furthermore, my memory and interpretation of an event will not be the same as yours, especially if there is a point of contention. The fundamental attribution error (FAE) will severely affect the meaning each of us attaches to an event. FAE is one's natural tendency to use dispositional or personality-based explanations when interpreting another's behavior and discounting situational influences. You tend to do the opposite for your own behavior, basing your explanation on your intentions and situational factors.

Bailey didn't get her report done on time because she procrastinates and is not motivated to do good work. Your report was late because Henry didn't provide you with the data you needed when it was due. This is the fundamental attribution error in action. You are keenly aware of your own internal dialogue, intentions, motivations and external environmental constraints. You don't have access to all this information to explain other's behavior, so you rely on character or personality judgements.

Added to this, the reticular activating system (RAS) will ensure that there will always be a difference between your description of an event and the other person's memory for that same event. This happens even if the FAE doesn't come into play, which it always does! Your RAS is continuously filtering all stimuli so what reaches your conscious brain for processing is not likely to be the same set of data that reaches the other party's prefrontal cortex. We are naturally set up to interpret the same event differently.

If we have not learned to start with the facts, when we enter a conversation, we will immediately go to the meaning which we have attached to the event. While frustrated with your teenage son, you might say something like: "I'm tired of you not listening to me. I asked you to take out the trash and once again, you just kept on playing your video games. You just don't care about this family." Your son has another version of the same event: "Once again, you expect me to just drop everything and do whatever it is you want me to do. I fully intended to take out the trash, but I was in the middle of an intense game. If you had just given me a chance, I would have taken out the trash when the game was over." The difference between your version of the event and your son's version sets the two of you up for conflict.

Start with the facts and you have an objective starting point. Dad asked son to take out trash. Son was playing a video game when Dad made the request. Thirty minutes later the trash has not been taken out. Both father and son agree on the facts. Good start but it isn't enough.

Facts are facts but they don't really explain the feelings associated with the event. Our elephant, the emotional brain, is not satisfied with just the facts. More importantly, feelings are a part of the whole sequence and cannot be ignored any more than the objective facts can be denied. In this step of explaining your meaning, you are going to share what the facts add up to in your mind.

Returning to our young man and the trash, it might sound something like this: "I asked you to take out the trash half an hour ago and the trash is still here. I feel like you aren't listening to me and that you don't care about helping out around here." Notice that this message had the same content as the first version, "I'm tired of you not listening to me..." You deliver the same message but because you started with the facts, it is now clear what led up to the meaning you attached to the situation. By stating the facts first, it is now clearer to the other party how you arrived at your meaning or the story which you have attached to the event. They don't have to agree with your meaning, and they probably won't, but they can now see why you are thinking or feeling what you are thinking or feeling.

One thing I have noticed when I teach people to list their facts is that they then skip sharing the meaning which they attached to the facts. Before training, they started with their meaning and skipped the facts. After training, the situation is reversed, and they skip the meaning. I believe that they do this because they have the same concern which Sue had, that it might make things worse. Sharing your meaning is uncomfortable but skipping this step is just as problematic as the original pattern of skipping the facts.

The meaning is in your head and if it isn't shared, it's still in the room. Even if you don't verbalize your meaning, the other party can feel it and the result is that they don't trust the conversation. In addition, you feel like you haven't really been honest. The facts are only part of the story. You must share what those facts mean to you.

You could get a negative response to sharing your meaning and for this there are some important tools for neutralizing emotions. These are discussed in detail in step 6.

There are a couple of things to keep in mind when sharing your meaning: First, own your meaning. Say "I feel like..." or "I'm beginning to think..." Start with an "I" statement, and not, "You make me feel like...." Take responsibility for your thoughts and feelings but share them. Second, share your meaning as a thought or a feeling, and not as a fact. Use phrases like, "I'm beginning to think…" or, "I'm wondering" or, "It feels like…"or, "I might be…." By using tentative phrases, you are signaling that you are open to seeing or hearing something different. The combination of owning your meaning and being tentative in your statements will lessen the feeling of threat in the other person and encourage them to share their meaning, which is the next step.

Step 4: Ask for their meaning.

"Once you have shared your meaning, it's time to hear Beth's perspective. There is always more than one meaning that can be attached to any set of facts. What meanings might Beth attach to the set of facts you shared with her?"

"I don't know what you mean?"

"If you were Beth, how might you explain her suggestion that she would work with you?"

"Oh, now I see. Beth might say that she is feeling some pressure from her boss and feels like she needs to get things in order so that she can ease this pressure. Is that what you mean?"

"Exactly. What other meaning could be attached to your facts?"

"That's hard. Let me think. Maybe she realized that things have changed and wants to understand how the work gets done under these new conditions."

"Right, if you had to, you could probably come up with many more explanations."

Sue frowned and then said, "Aren't I just making excuses for Beth?"

"No," I responded, "What you are doing is opening yourself to the possibility there is another valid explanation. You may be right in the first meaning you attached to the facts but there may be more to the story. How would you know?"

"I guess I would have to ask."

"Exactly! Before you can begin problem-solving, you need to understand Beth's meaning or you might be solving the wrong problem. If you don't give Beth a chance to challenge your meaning, it's like telling her you that you **know** your meaning is the truth. That, my friend, is guaranteed to make the conflict much worse."

How you ask for the other person's meaning is important. Choose from any of the following phrases to get the additional information which might change how you proceed and avoid moving on to problem-solving too early.

- What's your perspective on this?
- How do you see it?
- Is there something I'm missing?
- What are your thoughts on this?
- Help me understand…

The simpler the question, the better. You want to steer clear of the word "why" because it will trigger defensiveness and you absolutely want to avoid asking for a solution just yet.

When Sue had her talk with Beth, she listed off her facts and shared with Beth that she felt she was going to get fired. Beth was clearly surprised by Sue's concern, "Sue, given how upset I was the other day, I can see now how you might be thinking that. But it's very far from the truth. I've seen you working late every night for the last two months and I am concerned. We are about to take on a new project and I'm worried that you are worn out now. If I don't figure out some way to get you some help, there is no way you can handle this project and you are the only one who has the right expertise."

Beth's response was an eye-opener for Sue!

These conversations don't always work out the way it did for Sue. When approached properly, however, they always result in a good outcome. In Sue's case, mistrust quickly shifted to feeling valued and as a result of Beth's response the focus of the conversation took a very different turn. When you ask for the other party's meaning, it frequently does change the direction of the conversation. Sometimes you get additional information, sometimes you get a different perspective, and sometimes you get validation that the meaning you attached was correct. When you take the time to ask for the other person's meaning, it demonstrates that you respect their experience and it gives you an opportunity to re-think your meaning.

Step 5: Neutralize / Next Steps

Sometimes, as was the case for Beth and Sue, you can go directly to next steps which focuses on planning. More often, steps 3 and 4 have created emotions that must be calmed before you can engage in rational problem solving.

Neutralize emotions:

One reason why people often avoid sharing their meaning is because the meaning they attached to the facts is rarely positive. When they share it, the other party can become defensive, aggressive, accusatory, or simply withdraw from the conversation. None of that feels good. We may be anxious to get the difficult conversation behind us, but if we move too fast to the next step of solving the problem, we will not be able to negotiate a result that works well for both parties. Instead, we will be right back where we started. Sharing your meaning has triggered the other party's stress response and their response has prompted some level of alarm in your brain.

When you observe a negative response after you shared your meaning, you need to stop and use any of the safety tools discussed earlier. Listening can be difficult because what the other person says to us often feels like an attack. If you can listen without responding defensively, this burst of negativity will usually wear itself out in 3-5 minutes. Those few minutes of listening to what are often harsh words will feel like an eternity but, like a balloon losing its air, it will fizzle out. When you don't respond with anything but listening, the other party's energy has nothing to fuel it and then it often loses power until there is almost nothing. Once this happens, the principle of reciprocity comes into effect. Since you showed them the respect of listening, there is a greater probability that they will be willing to listen to you. The key is to be disciplined and to truly listen.

Listening does not mean you say nothing. Good listening is active. Listening with CARE is going to help you to truly understand and help the other person feel that they are being heard. CARE is an acronym for **C**larity, **A**ssure, **R**ephrase, and **E**ncourage.

Get *clarity* by asking open-ended questions to make sure that you understand what is being said. "Why" questions will provoke defensiveness but what, when, where, how questions are fine. I often use questions like, "When you said ___, did you mean ___?" or, "What does the word ___ mean to you?" or, "How does ___ feel to you?"

Assuring involves verbalizing your feelings for the other person, "I care about you," "I really want for us to be able to trust each other," or "I respect your knowledge on this issue." Obviously, don't say it if you don't believe it. Verbalizing positive regard is going to stimulate the release of DOSE neurotransmitters - dopamine, oxytocin, serotonin, and endorphins, in both your own and the other person's brain. Looking for something positive you can say with honesty will tone down the intensity of the interaction. Assuring can also include validating the other person's perspective. Validating doesn't mean you agree, it just means that you can see the logic of the thought or feeling. For example, "If those were the facts I had, I would have come to the same conclusion" or "If I had experienced what you did, I might have felt the same way."

Rephrasing helps the other person recognize that you are really listening and that you understand what they have said. When I tell someone something and they say that they understand, I don't believe them. In fact, in my mind I am answering, "No you don't!" On the other hand, if they can put what I have just said into their own words, I feel like they do understand. Rephrasing takes focus but, when you succeed, you get a "two-for-one" reward. First, the other person feels respected and understood which contributes to a sense of connectedness. Second, the rephrase can work in the same way as a clarifying question. If you missed the point, it will be obvious, and the meaning can be corrected immediately.

Encouraging gives the other person the courage to share their meaning. Simple nods and filler words like "and" can encourage the speaker to continue and to explain more fully. While encouragement is always useful, it is critical when the other person has withdrawn from the conversation. After you have shared your meaning and you ask for their meaning, it is not unusual for the other party to respond with silence or make movements to leave, or just say something like: "I have nothing to say" or "If that's how you feel, then there's no point in my talking." When that happens, a comment from you like, "I really want to hear your perspective" or "Please, I really want to listen," can make a big difference in getting the other person to share what they are thinking and feeling.

Next Steps:

Once you have worked your way through the first five steps and, if necessary, neutralized any negative emotions that may have been aroused, you can now problem-solve. This is the easiest part of the CLEAN/N process. Both you and the other person can think clearly, you have built an honest understanding of each other's perspectives and, as a result, you are now focused on the right problem and are motivated to find a solution. The bonus is that when you solve the right problem, the solution tends to hold. Today's solution is less likely to become tomorrow's problem.

I like to use the following formula to pose the problem that needs to be solved. How do we [*accomplish my objective*] while also [*accomplishing your objective*]. The formula works just as well if you reverse the order by first stating the other person's objective and then your own. When I put the problem statement front and center in this way, it sets the framework for finding a both/and instead of an either/or solution.

Toolkit Summary

- Most difficult conversations can be solved with less direct tools but for conflict that has risen to the level of dispute or discord, the CLEAN/N approach is needed.

- The CLEAN/N approach is more effective when the less direct tools are integrated with it.

- Starting by asking permission to talk demonstrates respect and gives the other party some sense of control.

- Creating and maintaining safety is essential to the success of the CLEAN/N approach.

- There are four safety tools: demonstrating caring, apologizing, establishing mutual purpose, and contrast statements.

- Listing facts creates a base of agreement.

- Explaining your meaning shares with the other person what the facts mean to you.

- Asking for their meaning helps you to understand their perspective and improves the probability of solving the right problem.

- The fundamental attribution error (FAE) and the reticular activating system (RAS) ensure that your perspective is not going to be the same as that of the other person.

- Neutralizing emotions is necessary before problem solving can begin.

- Finally, "Next steps" is to develop a solution that works for both parties.

Executing the Plan

It's time to use all these tools to improve the quality of our more difficult conversations with others. In the past, it seemed like there were only two choices. You could get what you want by dominating or demanding and that would damage a relationship. Something to keep in mind, in a relationship, if one person loses, no one wins. In the short-term it might feel like you won, but the damage done to a relationship will, in the end, hurt you. The other choice is to preserve the relationship by avoiding the conflict. Your own experience tells you that this approach never works. You feel stressed and the resentment builds. The other person continues doing whatever it is that is upsetting you and then, one day, it explodes. When it does, the conflict is much worse than if it had been dealt with when it first showed up. The tools described in this book can help you have the proverbial "cake and eat it, too." You can get a good result AND nurture important relationships. The next chapter will offer a couple of methods that will help you use these tools more effectively.

12

Using the Tools

Choosing your tools

Every day brings with it some degree of stress and often some level of conflict. I was out for a Saturday run with my husband. For a July day, the temperature was mild and there was a slight mist falling, just enough to make the temperature even more comfortable. We were running beside a lovely lake that was dotted with a few canoes sitting peacefully while the occupants fished or napped. The morning couldn't have been more calming. Feeling great after a good run, we get into the car and head for our after-run treat, breakfast at our favorite morning restaurant. And then it happened – we made a wrong turn and, attempting to right the situation, made another wrong turn. I would like to say I handled it wonderfully but my husband will tell you otherwise. Even on such a perfect day, conflict creeped in.

Conflict has a nasty habit of getting bigger if we don't deal with it when it shows up. The previous chapters provided a smorgasbord of tools that you can use to deal with conflict and on the surface, this appears to be a good thing. More choice is better, right? Barry Schwartz, in his book, *The Paradox of Choice*,[12] explained that too much choice can be paralyzing. When faced with too many choices, we tend to shut down and not make any choice at all and in the case of conflict, this is a problem. If you don't decide, a decision will be made for you and you probably won't like the resolution.

We need a way of simplifying how we choose between the many different tools so that we don't feel overwhelmed by them. The Matrix of Conflict Management Tools below sorts the tools according to the effort needed to implement them and whether the focus of the tool is on changing your behavior/feelings or changing the behavior/feelings of others.

Figure 3: Matrix of Conflict Management Tools

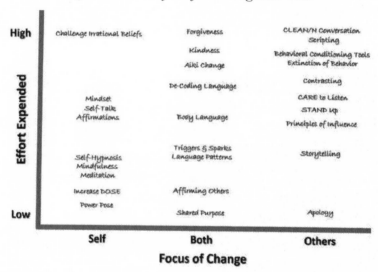

The following is a set of questions which, combined with the matrix, will help you to select the tools you want to use.

1. Will this conflict take care of itself if I just wait?

Some issues will resolve themselves if we just wait. The tension between my husband and me disappeared as soon as we found our way to the restaurant and coffee was served. Apologies were certainly merited and once offered, the situation was resolved. Some conflict between two people is inevitable and not all situations require an active intervention.

However, be sure to watch for patterns developing. Minor irritations can build hurts and resentment when they become a pattern. It is important to understand the difference between once-off issues, which can be allowed to resolve themselves and a pattern of behavior which should be addressed.

2. How stressed am I feeling about this situation?

Things happen that aren't exactly the way you intended or wished them to be. When this happens, you can check in with yourself to gauge the level of stress you are feeling. Rate your stress on a 10-point scale. A rating of 1 to 3 is low enough for you to take a wait and see approach. You might choose to be proactive and think about using one or two of the tools which do not require a lot of effort to implement. When you use low effort tools the tension associated with the situation can often be eliminated almost magically.

If your stress rating is at a 4 to 7, you might find your thoughts wandering back to the issue and maybe you are even feeling some physical symptoms like sleep disruption or headaches. Once this is the case, it's time to get more serious about using some tools. You don't have to use all the tools, but the more tools you combine, the bigger the impact. You might put more emphasis on those tools that require mid-level effort and select a combination of tools from the 'Both' column in the Matrix of Conflict Management Tools.

If your stress level is at an 8 to 10, it's time for a comprehensive approach. At this level you will certainly need the tools that require more effort. Chances are that you will need to have a CLEAN/N conversation, combined with some safety tools and the liberal use of CARE listening (Clarity, Assurance, Rephrase and Encouraging).

3. Where is this situation on the conflict continuum?

Feelings of stress can be subtle, and we don't always have sufficient self-awareness to rate our stress level accurately. Another way to choose which tools to use is to decide where on the conflict continuum the situation lies. If the conflict is at the level of irritation, worry/troubled, or misunderstanding, then any of the tools requiring less effort are going to be helpful. Mix and match according to what you feel comfortable with. If you aren't seeing a result with one approach, either change to another one or add something else to what you are already doing.

If the conflict is at the level of disagreement or argument, you can start by using a combination of the low- and mid-level effort tools. At this level you will probably need to combine tools from both ends of the focus continuum, focusing on change within yourself and in others. If you are not seeing a needed change, then it might be time to use a CLEAN/N conversation.

Once a situation has risen to the level of dispute or discord, it's time to take a comprehensive approach. At this level you will need to combine several of the mid- and high-level effort tools with a CLEAN/N conversation. When conflict has risen to this level, it is worth taking some time to really understand the situation and then decide on how best to approach it.

For most disputes you get to choose when you initiate a CLEAN/N conversation. There will be times, however, when you are blindsided by a dispute. When this happens, you will rarely handle it well. Fortunately, we can usually create a do-over. Take some time to review what happened, how you responded, and how you wished you had responded. You can then implement the CLEAN/N conversation, beginning with that very important "can we talk" step. Whether you are choosing when to have a conversation or planning a do-over, some preparation will improve the outcome dramatically. This is where scripting comes in.

The power of scripting

As discussed throughout this book, a major challenge for managing conflict is that our emotions can easily become elevated. You might be calm and focused at the start of the conversation but then something is said, and your hands start sweating and your heart rate speeds up. Breathing will help but sometimes this is not enough to manage the surging stress response. Your ability to think clearly deteriorates rapidly under these circumstances. This is where scripting becomes useful. It takes much less mental energy to recall a response than to construct one.

While you are calm and able to think clearly, you can consider how you will ask for the conversation and what your response would be if the person is not willing to talk. Listing your facts will give you an opportunity to organize the sequence of events in your mind and to review your facts for potential added meaning. Writing down what your facts mean to you allows you to look at the meaning from a more dissociated perspective and occasionally, this alone will change the meaning for you. This might then alter the conversation or even eliminate the need for a conversation. Predicting how the other person might respond when you share your meaning isn't rocket science and this helps you to plan which safety tools you will use. Contrast statements will come naturally after you have practiced using them, but it always helps to compose a couple in advance.

Once you have your script, you can review it just before having the CLEAN/N conversation and then put it away. This will help to remind you of your intentions before entering the conversation. It will also ensure that the content is fresh in your mind, helping to improve your recall. However, you don't want to memorize the script because then you will come across as inauthentic. Furthermore, despite your plans, the conversation is unlikely to follow your script exactly. It is better to think of the script as a resource that you can draw on and adjust as necessary. Preparing the script for your difficult conversation simply reduces the amount of mental energy you will need to expend while striving to stay focused and respond to the other person in the most productive way possible.

A template for the script would include the following:

Context – [What is the situation?]

Can we talk – [How will you ask for the conversation?]

Safety tools – [What safety tools will be used, if needed and how will they be worded?]

Facts – [What are all the facts and which ones will I use in the conversation?]

Share my meaning – [What do these facts mean to me? What am I feeling or thinking?]

Ask for their meaning – [How will I ask for their meaning?]

Neutralize negativity – [In addition to using CARE to listen, which safety tools might I need and how will they be worded?]

Toolbox Summary

- When you have too many choices, it can result in indecision.
- Use the Matrix of Conflict Management Tools to select tools based on effort and focus for change.
- Ask yourself three questions to determine which tools are the most appropriate: Will the situation resolve itself? How stressed am I about the situation? And, where on the conflict continuum does this situation fall?
- If you are going to use the CLEAN/N tool, script the conversation in advance.

13

Blindsided

Blindsided: take one – in person

I had just returned from lunch and Ryan was sitting in my office. In my head, I quickly ran through my day's schedule and no, I didn't recall a meeting with Ryan. That didn't mean anything because it wasn't unusual for me to forget a meeting. Taking a second look, however, it was clear that this meeting was not going to be a pleasant one. Ryan's body language said it all. His body was stiff, and his hands were firmly gripping the arms of the chair. When he turned to look at me, his face was red, and his jaw was clenched. What was all this about? We had always worked well together. Why was Ryan so upset?

Before I had a chance to say anything, Ryan blurted out, "I heard what you said about me to Kendra."

Now I was really confused, "What I said about you to Kendra?"

"Yes, you told her I wouldn't get the Jethro project done on time. You know d---#&$% well I've been working night and day on that project and the only reason it won't get done is because **you** aren't getting **your** data to me on time. I don't appreciate you throwing me under the bus – if the project doesn't get done on time, it's your fault and not mine."

My heart started beating fast and I could feel the hairs on the back of my neck rising as my body heated up.

"That isn't what I said to Kendra. I told her…"

"Kendra told me exactly what you said, and I am fed up with you. This project means a lot to me and I'm not going to let you make me responsible for the delay. Don't expect a whole lot of help from me or my team from here on out."

With that, he got up and stormed out of my office. With my body shaking, I stood there in shock. It took a minute or two before I unclenched my hands and sat down. How could this have gone so wrong? Yes, I did tell Kendra that the project wasn't going to meet the deadline, but I know I hadn't blamed Ryan. My team had run into some roadblocks and Ryan was right, we hadn't gotten him the data he needed. How do I make this right? Do I even want to make it right? Ryan had no business attacking me like that and maybe I should let him, and his team take the blame. Afterall, the last time we worked on a project together, his team gave me some wrong data and my team had looked bad. It was just like him – he always looks for ways to blame others.

I really wanted to go after Ryan and give him a piece of my mind. I didn't appreciate his just showing up and tearing into me in that way. I couldn't believe he would think so poorly of me. After all the times I had covered for him, how could he treat me like this? Instead of chasing Ryan down, I walked over to my friend Amy and told her all about what had just happened. As expected, Amy agreed that Ryan was out of line. Feeling better, I went back to my office with a firm intention to avoid ever working with Ryan on any project ever again!

Blindsided: take two – keyboard courage

It was a Tuesday morning when I opened my email to a message from Lilly with the subject line: *Eljay Report*. Curious, I opened the message:

I see you have taken over this report. I have been working on
it for two weeks now. I don't appreciate your just stepping in
without even discussing it with me. If you don't have enough
to do, you might discuss it with Sam. It isn't fair that you just
cherry-pick the assignments you like and ignore the work the
rest of us are doing. Some of us try to be team-players. You
might try it.

Wow, I felt punched in the gut. A host of thoughts were flooding
through my mind and none of them were very kind. Lilly was usually
an amiable, kind person. Where was this coming from? I quickly wrote
back:

Lilly, I had no idea that you were working on the Eljay report.
I didn't, as you put it, "cherry-pick" this assignment. Sam gave
it to me, so your issue is with him, not me. Maybe you should
keep Sam informed of the work you are doing. Or, are you
exempt from having to report to him the way the rest of us do?

Keying that email felt good. I felt fully justified to give Lilly back the
same lack of respect which she had shown to me! Keyboard courage
was easy. Fortunately, I deleted the email before I sent it. Yay, me! But
that didn't stop me from walking right past Lilly in the cafeteria
without greeting her and I certainly didn't look her way in the staff
meeting that afternoon. I just let the email hang and didn't make any
effort to correct Lilly's assumptions. Furthermore, I felt justified in
avoiding her and treating her with the same lack of respect with which
I felt she was treating me.

Blindsided: take three – I am the blindsider

I pulled up outside of the back door of my building. My office was on
this side of the building, so it just made sense to go in through the back
door. There, sitting at a picnic bench, were two employees, smoking.
Our company has a strict rule of no smoking anywhere on company
grounds rule. I could pretend not to see it and go about my business
or I could do something about it. Just ignoring the behavior didn't feel
right so I walked over and, with a tentative voice said,

"You know, the rule against smoking includes anywhere on company
grounds."

The taller of the two responded, "We're outside. We aren't bothering anyone."

"The rule is, anywhere on company grounds," I said with a little more force.

The other employee responded, "Our supervisor knows we are smoking out here and she doesn't care. It's a stupid rule."

"Really!" was all I said. I headed straight for my office and fired off emails to the employees' supervisor, and their division's manager, director and VP. Just for good measure, I also sent an email detailing the situation to my VP and to the VP of HR. I was hot and I was going to make sure these two girls and their supervisor were properly reprimanded! Instead of dealing with the conflict directly, I resorted to using my authority and keyboard courage. Not the best route for future dealings with either of these employees or their immediate supervisor.

Blindsiding happens

The term blindsided comes from football when the quarterback is attacked from the direction opposite to where he is looking. In the business world, blindsided means you are caught off-guard and unprepared; attacked from an unexpected position. In the first two examples, I was surprised by what I felt were unfair, personal attacks. In the third example, I was on the attack and feeling quite justified. In all three cases, relationships had been damaged and needed repair.

When situations like these go unchecked, they are going to lead to further misunderstandings and discord. They aren't good for the parties involved and they are not good for the organization. You probably have plenty of your own examples of similar unpleasant and perhaps dysfunctional interactions. Sadly, it would be unusual if you didn't.

Up to now our discussion on how to approach conflict has been based on the premise that you can prepare yourself for dealing with it. With proper preparation, you can keep your emotions in check, and, with the right approach, you can work through the conflict and arrive at a productive result. While this is true for most conflicts, a conflict sometimes comes out of nowhere and soon both you and the other party experience raging negative emotions. What do you do in situations like this?

Blindsided and discounting the future

There is no magic formula for managing a blindsided conflict. It is a given that no one behaves admirably when this happens. The first priority when you find yourself blindsided is to minimize the amount of damage that will need to be cleaned up later. The second priority is not to allow the situation to slip away from you and fester into something bigger. A blindsided conflict must be dealt with; but it can rarely be effectively when it is addressed in the moment. This kind of situation requires a little "cooling-off" before it is dealt with.

The problem is that, once you have cooled off, you will be tempted to just let it go. You could end up paying a high price by letting it go because you will be "discounting the future." It's easy to convince ourselves that the unpleasantness of the conversation in the present outweighs the potential future gain of resolving the issue. Or, to describe it slightly differently, the cost of future discord between us and the other party will not be high enough to merit the effort it will take to improve our current relationship.

STAND up to a blindside

In the middle of a blindside, emotions are running high and you are in fight-or-flight mode. You just want the blindside to be over and you either focus on how to escape the situation, or you are in attack mode. Either response is not going to serve you well. A better response is to STAND up to the blindside: **S**top; **T**ake a breath; **A**ctively listen; **N**eutralize emotions; and, **D**ecide.

Stop:

As soon as your heart starts beating faster, your brain is in perfect synchrony and shifts up to faster beta wave-lengths. Your best, most creative thinking occurs at the lower beta wavelengths. The shift to a higher frequency allows you to think faster but it compromises your problem-solving ability. Resist the urge to act immediately unless there is a clear and immediate danger. Remember that your first priority is not to make things worse than they already are. Give yourself a chance to slow down and re-engage your best thinking power.

Take a breath

When you stop, remind yourself to breathe. Obviously, you are going to breathe. However, when you have been blindsided, your breathing is going to become faster and shallower. In addition, with your fight-or-flight mode activated, your body is moving blood and oxygen away from the brain to the rest of the body to prepare for running or fighting. This leaves less oxygen available to the brain for thinking. You can mitigate or even reverse this action by taking some deep breaths. It will also help to slow down your heartbeat and brainwaves. Breathe mindfully by counting to three on the inhale and exhale to a count of four. Repeat this at least three times, and a few more times if you can.

Actively listen

Stopping and breathing pair well with actively listening. That doesn't mean you don't say anything, but it does mean that you do **not** defend yourself or argue a point made by the other party. Given that the other party is probably in fight-or-flight mode, much of what they have to say is going to feel like an attack or an inaccurate twisting of facts. They have attached meaning to the facts and their meaning is not the same as yours. Listen, because if you do, you will learn, and it might even change your understanding of the situation.

Listening will do three things. First, you may get additional details that were missing from your version of what happened, and you will certainly gain some insight as to how the other party is seeing and feeling about the situation. Second, if you don't resist their account and just allow it to play out, the other party runs out of steam. If you don't feed their anger or frustration, the other party literally runs out of things to say. This usually happens within three to five minutes, albeit a very long three to five minutes for you. If you can be patient, you will get your turn to speak and when you do, the other party will be calmer. This brings us to the third advantage that comes with listening. You have shown respect to the other party by listening. This is a gift, and the principle of reciprocity says that it is a social norm to return to others any positive actions which they have given to us. If we listen first, the chance of the other party being willing to listen to us in return improves greatly.

Use the CARE to listen model while actively listening. Get clarity by asking open-ended, clean questions. It is essential that you don't assume that you understand what the other party is saying, particularly when code words are being used. Assure the other party that you care about them and/or that you care about resolving the situation to everyone's advantage. If appropriate, you can validate their feelings. Rephrase key ideas in their argument to demonstrate that you understand. Sometimes just repeating a short phrase with no additional comment can achieve this goal. Finally, encourage the other party to continue talking, even if you wish they would stop, with simple nods, filler words or assurances that you want to hear what they have to say.

Neutralize emotions

If the other party is present, you can work on calming emotions. Sometimes this opportunity is not immediately present because the blindside came via a written email or memo or the other person exited the situation immediately after delivering the attack. Neutralizing emotions must be done in person or, if that is not possible, with video conferencing or at the least, by telephone. Any attempt at neutralizing emotions via the written word is hazardous because without tonality and body language, the words can easily be misunderstood.

Neutralizing emotions will need a mix of several tools. You can apologize, if you have something to apologize for. That may take a little humility on your part. It's never easy to admit to yourself or to others that you are not the innocent victim. You can also assure the other person that you care about them, or that you share a mutual purpose with them. Finally, you can use a contrast statement to reduce their sense of threat and to clarify your intentions.

Decide on next steps

You may not be able to neutralize emotions because the other party is simply not available or because emotions are running too high. Sometimes people just need some time before they can see things from a more objective perspective. If you are not able to neutralize emotions, then a decision should be made about when and where a future conversation will take place. If you don't make the commitment and schedule the meeting, you will convince yourself later that the conversation isn't necessary. Deciding that you don't have to have the conversation will eventually hurt you, so don't do it. Take some time to schedule a future conversation as soon as possible after the blindside.

If you have done the hard work of listening and you are then able to neutralize emotions, you are now ready to have a deep conversation. Use the CLEAN/N model. If you have been practicing other conversations by scripting, you will easily remember the critical steps and be able to apply them. This model will serve you well. If you get part way into the conversation and find that emotions are beginning to build, return to the safety tools. **Do not** try to resolve the issue if either party is in fight-or-flight mode. Rational thinking is seriously compromised whenever negative emotions are dominating. Quality problem-solving can only occur when the rational, logical mind is fully engaged. When it is, you will be able to find a resolution that both parties are happy with and committed to.

Toolkit Summary

- The PPE model which involves preparing your emotions, planning your conversation and executing your plan, assumes that you can anticipate when and where a conflict will happen, but this is not always the case.
- When you are blindsided by a conflict, you need an immediate response.
- You can STAND up to a blindside:
    - Stop – wait for a minute or two before you respond.
    - Take a breath – get more oxygen into your system so that you can think more clearly.
    - Actively listen using CARE to listen.
    - Neutralize negative emotions
    - Decide on next steps:
        - When and where to have a deep discussion; or,
        - How to resolve the issue.

14

Making it Work

Getting results

Remi is a nurse in the emergency unit of a large metropolitan hospital. He had to work a shift without proper personal protective equipment (PPE) and five days later, his 12-year-old son became sick with Covid-19 and needed to be hospitalized. Remi's first inclination was to rant at his supervisor about the situation. He felt that he and his son were victims and he wanted the hospital and his supervisor punished for the harm they had done. Fortunately for Remi, he didn't follow his first inclination but, instead, prepared a CLEAN/N script for a conversation with his supervisor.

"When I wrote my script, I realized that my supervisor and the hospital were also victims. They were working very hard to find more PPE but there was only so much they could do. That changed the conversation, entirely."

Remi went ahead and had the CLEAN/N conversation with his supervisor. The conversation didn't solve the PPE problem, but it did serve to build more trust between them. Remi came away from the conversation with a clear understanding of how much his supervisor cared about him, the team and all their families. For Remi, that meant a lot. The anger and frustration he had felt toward his supervisor and other hospital administrators had eased. Once he felt more connected, it was easier for Remi to support others who were dealing with the same demands.

Shane was frustrated when Antonio claimed another sale that should have been his. Shane had spent thirty minutes on the phone with the customer but then the customer was interrupted before he could finalize the sale. When she called back, Antonio picked up the call and closed the deal. This sort of thing kept happening and, if Shane was honest with himself, he might have done the same thing if he had been in Antonio's shoes.

Shane was tired of the animosity between himself and Antonio and he decided to try kindness for a couple of weeks to see what happened. He also kept track in a journal each time he used a trigger or a spark word or phrase. Much to his surprise two things happened. First, he and Antonio seemed to be talking more often and Antonio even suggested going for a drink after work. Second, after a few days of journaling, he slipped up less often with trigger words and he realized he was using more spark words.

"I decided to go out for that drink with Antonio and without expecting it, the conversation turned to the issue of sales. It came out that Antonio was feeling a lot of the same things I was, and he had some ideas on how to make more fair for both of us. Together we worked out a clearer understanding of who should get credit for which sales and when we would share credit for a sale. None of this would have happened if I had kept treating Antonio like he was the enemy."

Camille was thinking that she needed to quit her job. She liked the work and she was doing well but she felt that two of her co-workers were picking on her. Shelly and Pat ate lunch together which meant Camille had to cover the phones while they were gone. She didn't mind taking the later lunch but felt that they just took it for granted that she would. The week before, when she presented an idea at a team meeting, she felt as though Shelly and Pat were attacking her. Camille talked about the situation with her boss who told her she was reading too much into the incident. Camille began wondering if he might be right.

"I have always been an anxious person and my feelings get hurt pretty easily. I heard about meditation and thought it might help me think more clearly. I got started with that and created a self-affirmation that I can use any time things get stressful. I see things differently and feel much better. I even started talking with Pat and Shelly. I found out that when they question my ideas, it's because they just really want to make sure a change will help, not make things harder!"

The tools you choose to resolve conflict need to match the situation, the level of conflict, and your energy and what you feel comfortable with. It would be nice if there were a one-size-fits-all-situations solution, but this is not realistic when it comes to conflict. No two situations or people are alike, and this is why you need a range of different tools to choose from.

They aren't the enemy

What is the definition of insanity? According to an old saying, "insanity is doing the same thing and expecting a different result." Think about the way you have been handling conflict. Are you doing the same things you did in high school? Maybe you're a little more subtle about it now but, if you are being honest with yourself, you probably are. How well did it work when you were a kid? How well is it working now?

Getting angry and confronting the other person or just simply avoiding them didn't work well then and it's not working well now. When you are behaving in this way, you are treating the other person like the enemy. Give it enough time and they will become the enemy. It's a dance. They do something, you respond, they respond to your response, and on and on. If your intent is to win, their intent is not to let you win. In relationships, if one person loses, no one wins. This ugly dance needs to stop before it spirals down into a deep, black hole. The earlier you change your approach, the easier it is to turn a conflict around and find a more effective approach to resolving a difference.

Use the tools in this book. Mix and match according to the specific situation and what you feel most comfortable with. If one tool isn't getting you the results you want, try another. Better yet, combine tools.

Most importantly, keep trying. You deserve the results you need and want. You also deserve strong relationships with people who are important to you. Use these tools and continue to work on being a better version of you. You don't have to be perfect. Just keep working on it and I promise you, life gets easier, more fun, and your career will benefit.

Notes

1. Jonathan Haidt. *The Happiness Hypothesis: Finding Modern Truth in Ancient Wisdom.* (New York: Basic Books, 2006).

2. Kenneth W. Thomas and Ralph H. Kilmann. *Thomas-Kilmann Conflict Mode Instrument.* (Tuxedo, NY: Xicom, 1974).

3. Kerry Patterson, Joseph Grenny, Ron McMillan, and Al Switzler. *Crucial Conversations: Tools for Talking When Stakes Are High*, 2nd. Ed. (NY: McGraw-Hill Education, 2011).

4. Christopher Chabris and Daniel Simon. *The Invisible Gorilla: How Our Intuitions Deceive Us.* (Wexford, PA: Harmony, 2011).

5. Kelly McGonical. *The Willpower Instinct: How Self-Control Works, Why It Matters, and What You Can Do To Get More Of It.* (Garden City, NY: Avery, 2013).

6. John Medina. *Brain Rules: 12 Principles for Surviving and Thriving at Work, Home and School*, 2nd Ed. (Fall River, MA: Pear Press, 2014).

7. Robert Cialdini. *Influence: The Psychology of Persuasion*, Revised Ed. (NY: Harper Business, 2006).

8. Robert Enright. *Forgiveness is a Choice: A Step-by-Step for Resolving Anger and Restoring Hope.* (Washington, DC: APA LifeTools, 2019).

9. Wendy Sullivan and Judy Rees. *Clean Language: Revealing Metaphors and Opening Minds.* (Williston, VT: Crown House Publishing, 2008).

10. Amy Cuddy. *Presence: Bringing Your Boldest Self to Your Biggest Challenges.* (NY: Little, Brown, Spark, 2018).

11. Shawn Carson and Melissa Tiers. *Keeping the Brain in Mind: Practical Neuroscience for Coaches, Therapists and Hypnosis Practitioners.* (NY: Changing Mind, 2014).

12. Barry Schwartz. *The Paradox of Choice.* (NY: EccoPress, 2016.)

Another Book by

Dr. M. Paula Daoust

You can be calm and confident in a high-stakes speaking situation!

Are you stressed when faced with a high-stakes speaking situation? Do you feel short of breath or does your heart beat faster? When you must speak in front of others, do you notice your hands getting a little sweaty or is your stomach feeling queasy?

Imagine how your life would be different if you confidently embraced high-stakes speaking situations and performed at your best. How would your career improve if you could be calm and think clearly in these situations? With the tools in this book, you can discover for yourself how calm and confident you can be in any high-stakes speaking situation.

Available on Amazon.com!

Coming Soon!

January, 2021

Do you want to be average or a star-performer? This book will provide you with the tools to breakthrough to amazing sales success.

Using the latest brain science, you can use more brain power to see and take advantage of opportunities. With the tools and strategies in this book, you can create happy repeat customers and enjoy the entire sales process.

Watch for *Whole Brain Selling* and look forward to amazing sales success.

For more information, contact:

Dr. M. Paula Daoust

DrPaula@behaviortransitions.com

Made in the USA
Middletown, DE
13 July 2021